D E A D A G A I N

Will Pfeifer *writer* **Cliff Chiang** *artist and covers*
David Baron *colorist* **Rob Leigh** *letterer*
Based on ideas and characters developed by **Greg Rucka**

T H E C O L D H A N D O F V E N G E A N C E

David Lapham *writer* **Eric Battle** *penciller* **Prentis Rollins** *inker*
Guy Major *colorist* **Pat Brosseau** *letterer*

Mike Mignola & Dave Stewart **Neal Adams & Moose Baumann**
Michael Wm. Kaluta & David Baron **Matt Wagner & Dave Stewart**
original series covers

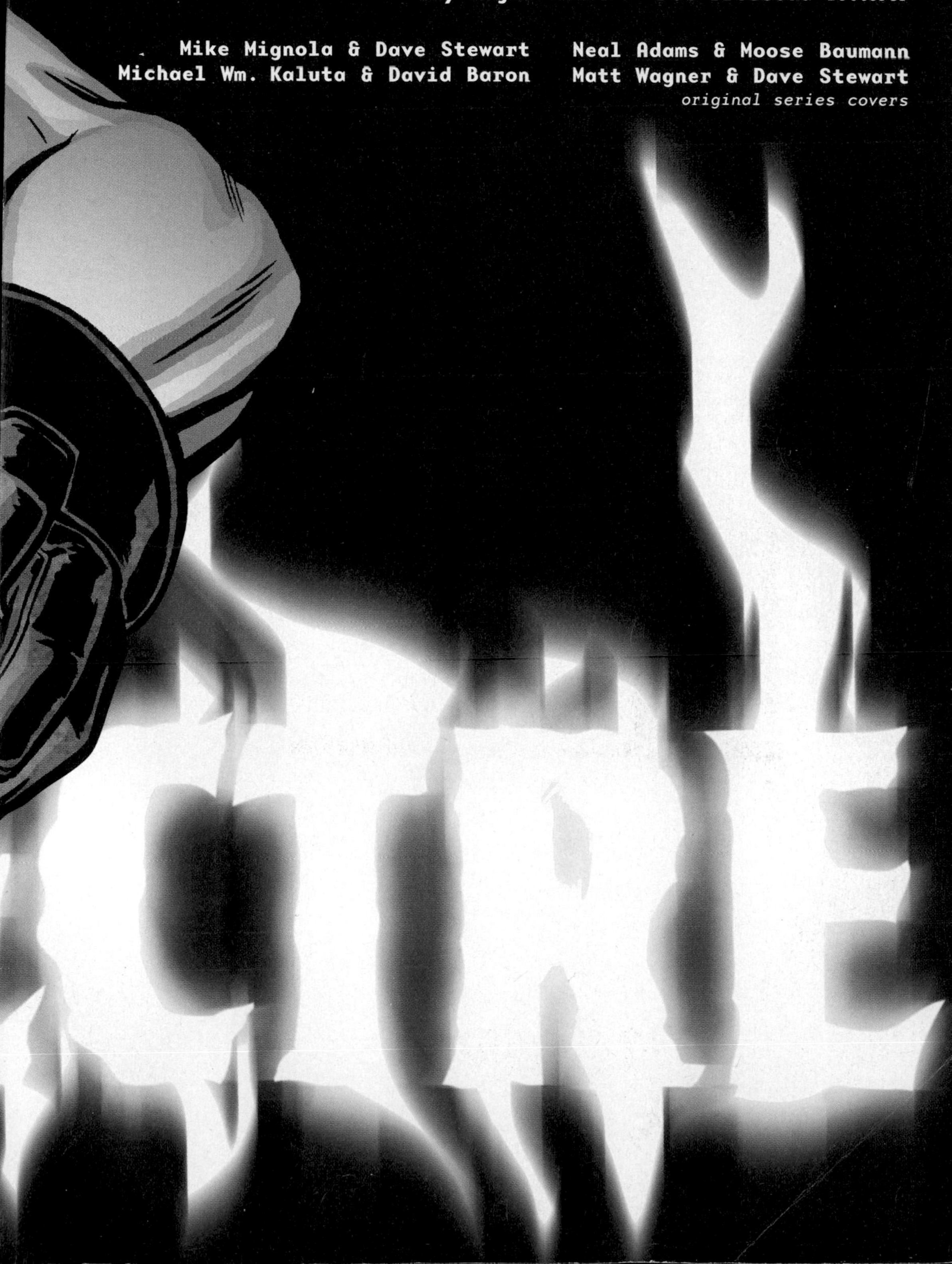

Dan DiDio Senior VP-Executive Editor
Matt Idelson, Bob Schreck Editors-original series
Nachie Castro Associate Editor-original series
Brandon Montclare Assistant Editor-original series
Peter Hamboussi Editor-collected edition
Robbin Brosterman Senior Art Director
Louis Prandi Art Director
Paul Levitz President & Publisher
Georg Brewer VP-Design & DC Direct Creative
Richard Bruning Senior VP-Creative Director
Patrick Caldon Executive VP-Finance & Operations
Chris Caramalis VP-Finance
John Cunningham VP-Marketing
Terri Cunningham VP-Managing Editor
Alison Gill VP-Manufacturing
Hank Kanalz VP-General Manager, WildStorm
Jim Lee Editorial Director-WildStorm
Paula Lowitt Senior VP-Business & Legal Affairs
MaryEllen McLaughlin VP-Advertising & Custom Publishing
John Nee VP-Business Development
Gregory Noveck Senior VP-Creative Affairs
Sue Pohja VP-Book Trade Sales
Cheryl Rubin Senior VP-Brand Management
Jeff Trojan VP-Business Development, DC Direct
Bob Wayne VP-Sales

Cover illustration by **Matt Wagner**
& **Dave Stewart**.

Crisis Aftermath: The Spectre
Published by DC Comics. Cover and
compilation copyright © 2007 DC Comics.
All Rights Reserved.

Originally published in single magazine
form in CRISIS AFTERMATH: THE SPECTRE
1-3 and TALES OF THE UNEXPECTED 1-3
© 2006, 2007 DC Comics. All Rights
Reserved. All characters, their
distinctive likenesses and related
elements featured in this publication
are trademarks of DC Comics. The
stories, characters and incidents
featured in this publication are
entirely fictional. DC Comics does not
read or accept unsolicited submissions
of ideas, stories or artwork.

DC Comics, 1700 Broadway,
New York, NY 10019
A Warner Bros. Entertainment Company
Printed in Canada. First Printing.
ISBN 1-4012-1380-4
ISBN 13 978-1-4012-1380-0

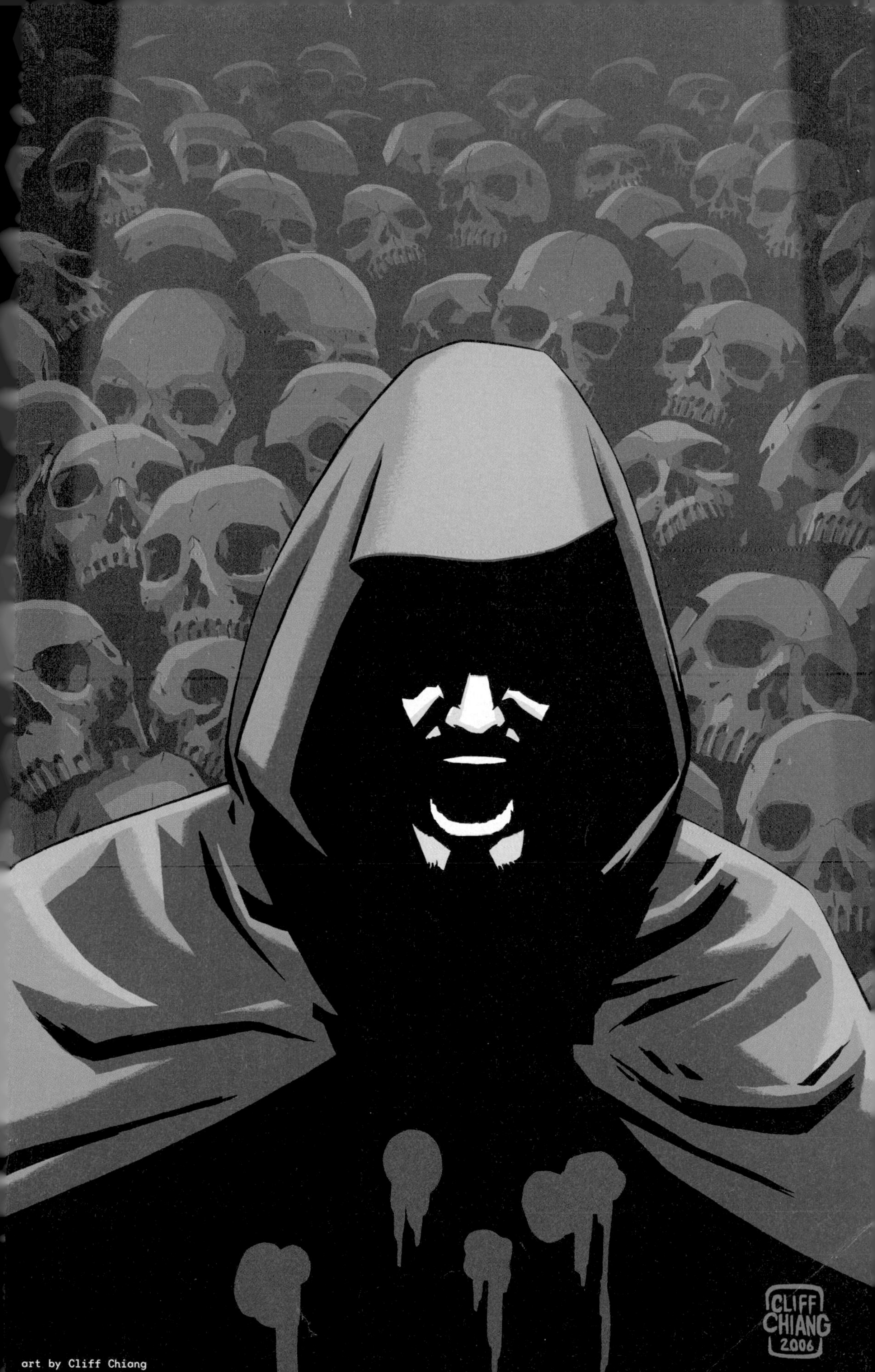
CLIFF CHIANG 2006
art by Cliff Chiang

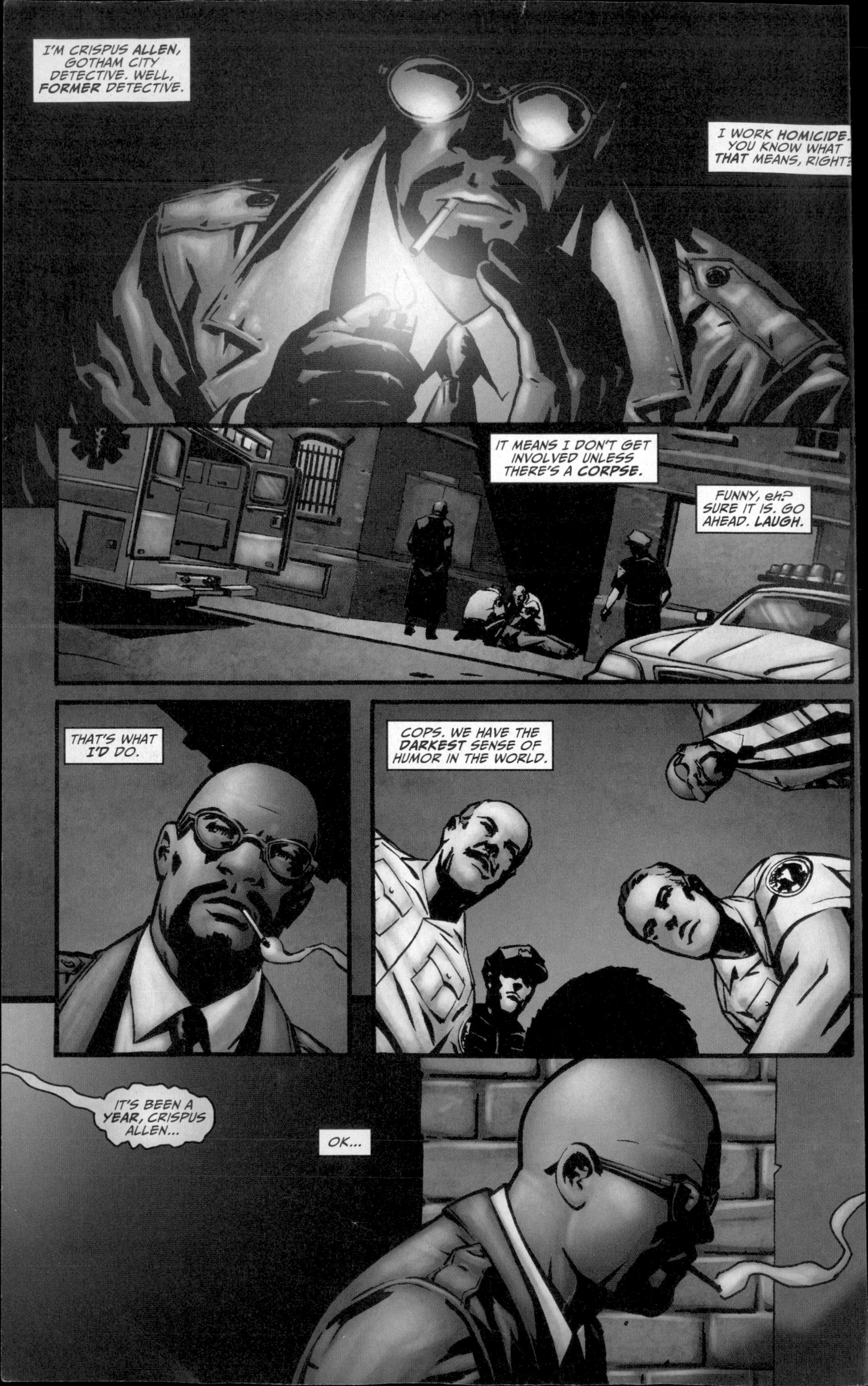
I'M CRISPUS ALLEN, GOTHAM CITY DETECTIVE. WELL, FORMER DETECTIVE.
I WORK HOMICIDE. YOU KNOW WHAT THAT MEANS, RIGHT?
IT MEANS I DON'T GET INVOLVED UNLESS THERE'S A CORPSE.
FUNNY, eh? SURE IT IS. GO AHEAD. LAUGH.
THAT'S WHAT I'D DO.
COPS. WE HAVE THE DARKEST SENSE OF HUMOR IN THE WORLD.
IT'S BEEN A YEAR, CRISPUS ALLEN...
OK...

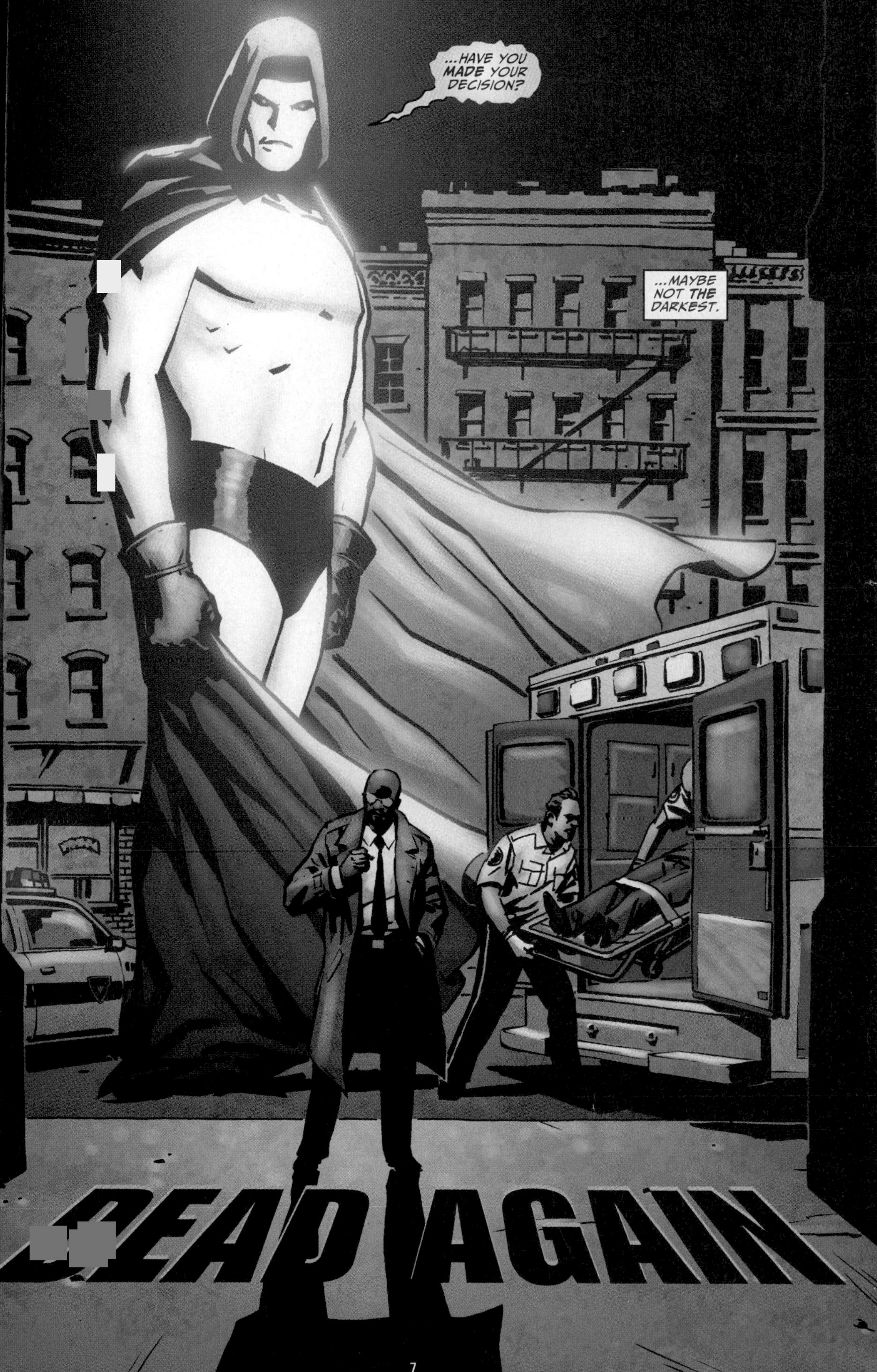
...HAVE YOU MADE YOUR DECISION?
...MAYBE NOT THE DARKEST.
DEAD AGAIN

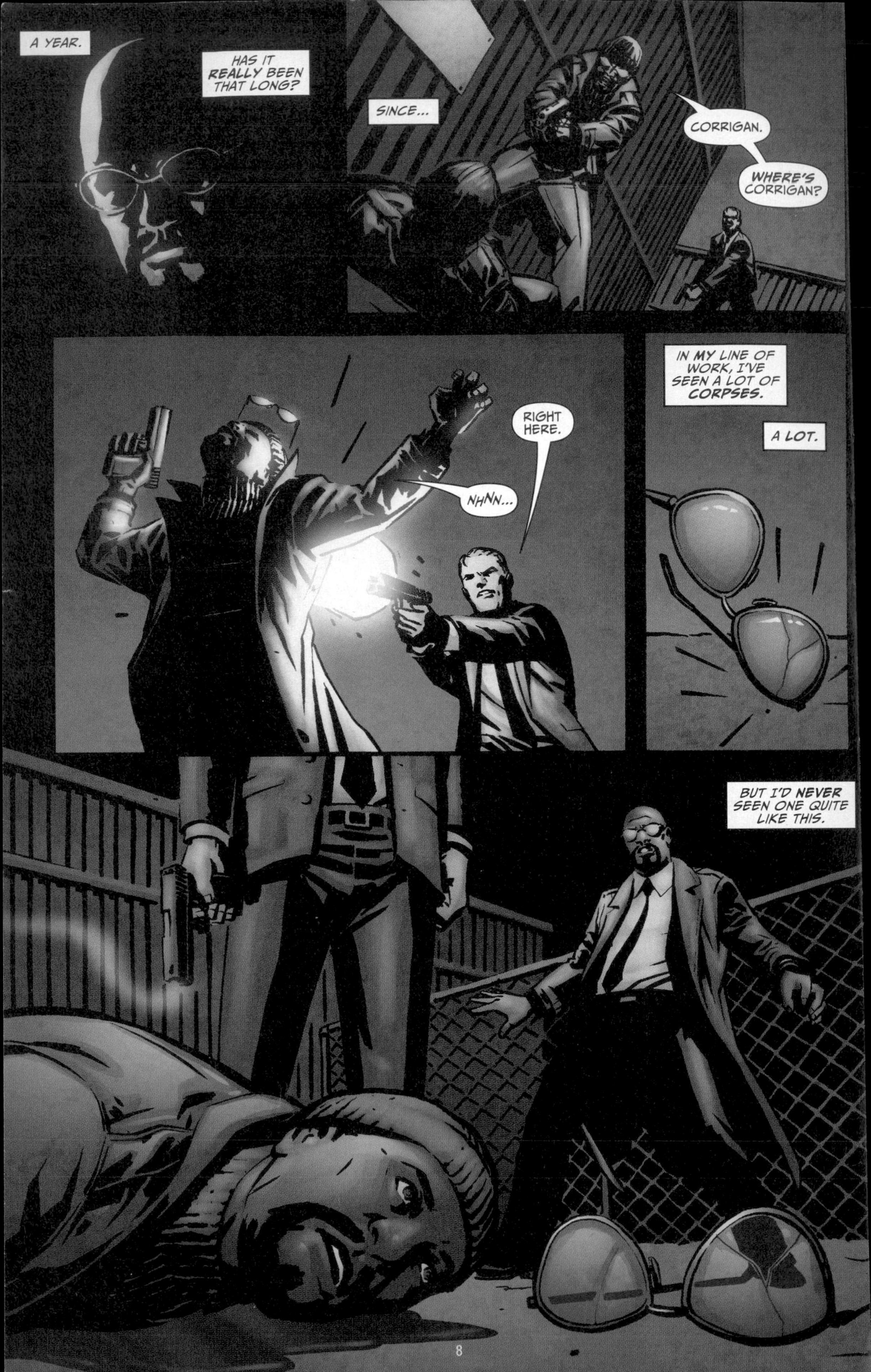
A YEAR.
HAS IT REALLY BEEN THAT LONG?
SINCE...
CORRIGAN.
WHERE'S CORRIGAN?
RIGHT HERE.
NHNN...
IN MY LINE OF WORK, I'VE SEEN A LOT OF CORPSES.
A LOT.
BUT I'D NEVER SEEN ONE QUITE LIKE THIS.

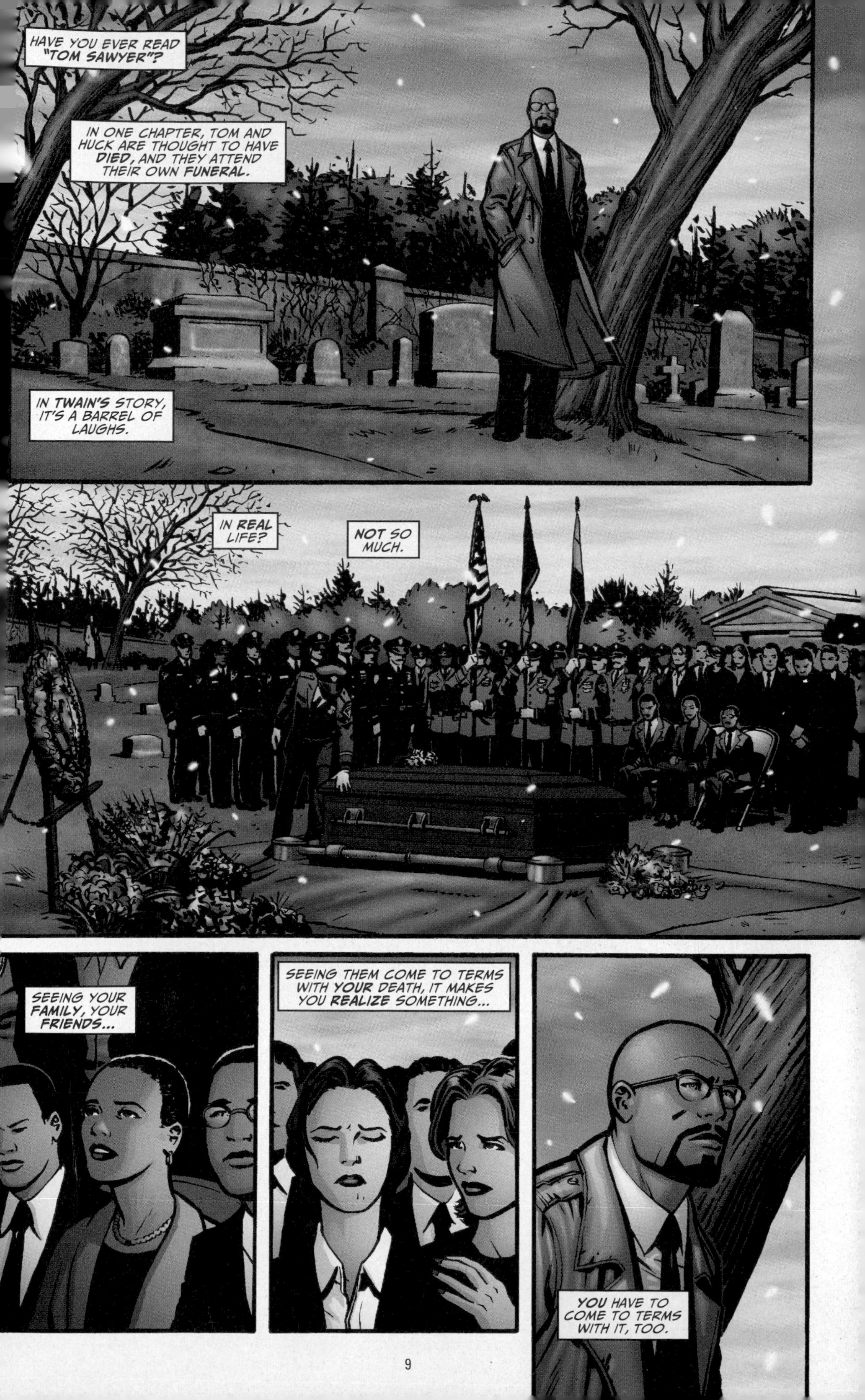
HAVE YOU EVER READ "TOM SAWYER"?
IN ONE CHAPTER, TOM AND HUCK ARE THOUGHT TO HAVE DIED, AND THEY ATTEND THEIR OWN FUNERAL.
IN TWAIN'S STORY, IT'S A BARREL OF LAUGHS.
IN REAL LIFE?
NOT SO MUCH.
SEEING YOUR FAMILY, YOUR FRIENDS...
SEEING THEM COME TO TERMS WITH YOUR DEATH, IT MAKES YOU REALIZE SOMETHING...
YOU HAVE TO COME TO TERMS WITH IT, TOO.

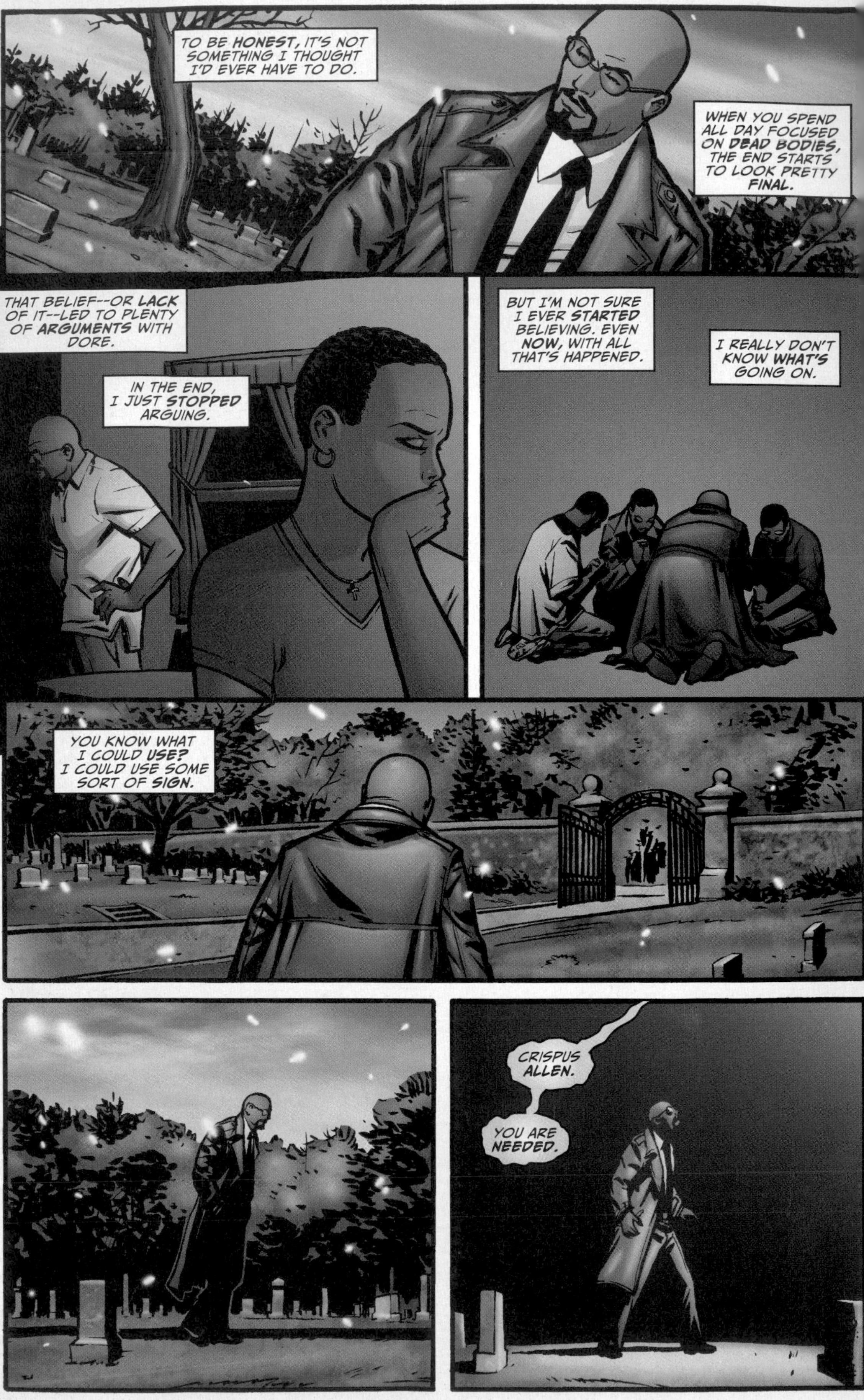
TO BE HONEST, IT'S NOT SOMETHING I THOUGHT I'D EVER HAVE TO DO.
WHEN YOU SPEND ALL DAY FOCUSED ON DEAD BODIES, THE END STARTS TO LOOK PRETTY FINAL.
THAT BELIEF--OR LACK OF IT--LED TO PLENTY OF ARGUMENTS WITH DORE.
IN THE END, I JUST STOPPED ARGUING.
BUT I'M NOT SURE I EVER STARTED BELIEVING. EVEN NOW, WITH ALL THAT'S HAPPENED.
I REALLY DON'T KNOW WHAT'S GOING ON.
YOU KNOW WHAT I COULD USE? I COULD USE SOME SORT OF SIGN.
CRISPUS ALLEN.
YOU ARE NEEDED.

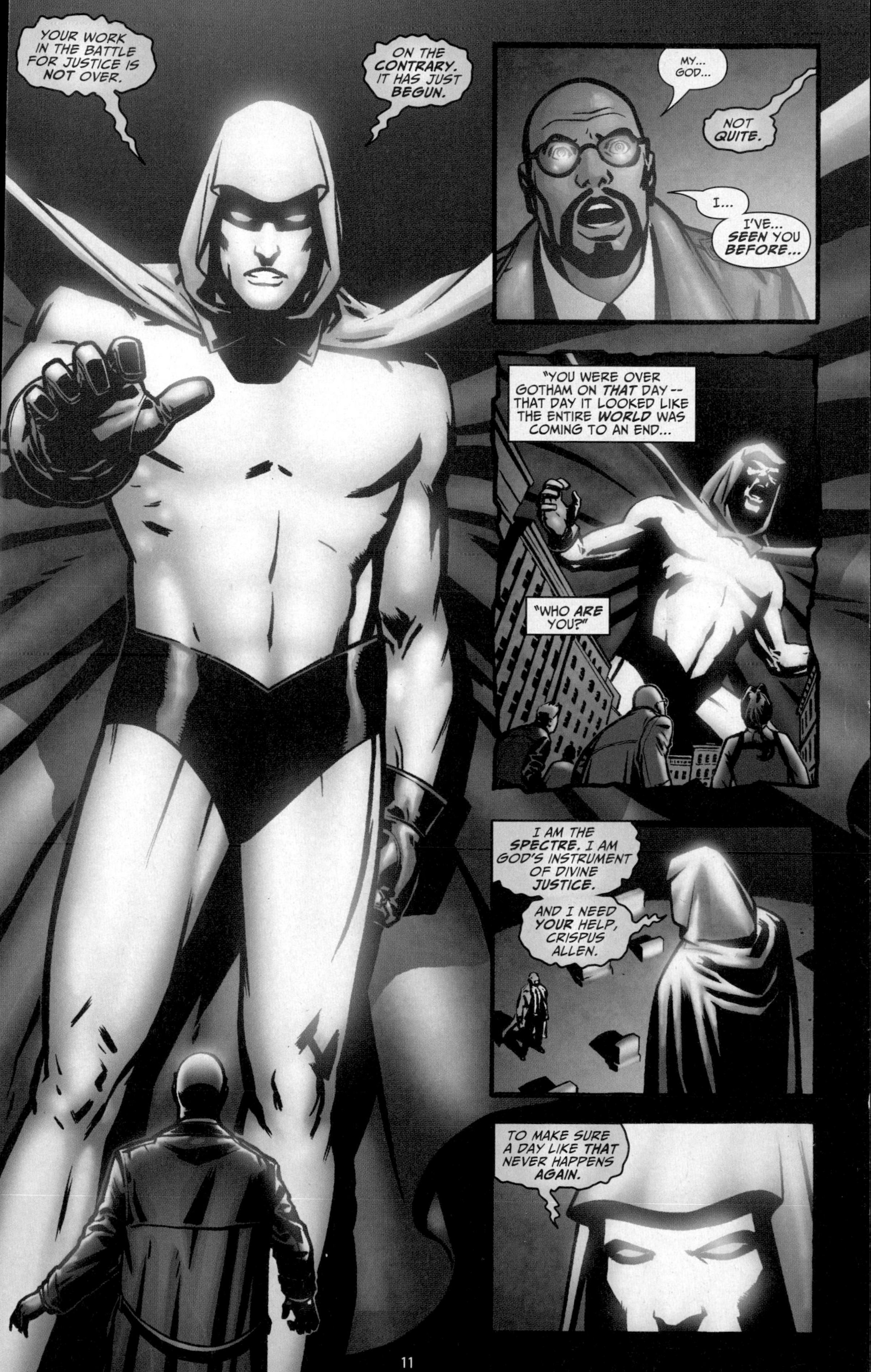
YOUR WORK IN THE BATTLE FOR JUSTICE IS NOT OVER.
ON THE CONTRARY. IT HAS JUST BEGUN.
MY... GOD...
NOT QUITE.
I...
I'VE... SEEN YOU BEFORE...
"YOU WERE OVER GOTHAM ON THAT DAY -- THAT DAY IT LOOKED LIKE THE ENTIRE WORLD WAS COMING TO AN END...
"WHO ARE YOU?"
I AM THE SPECTRE. I AM GOD'S INSTRUMENT OF DIVINE JUSTICE.
AND I NEED YOUR HELP, CRISPUS ALLEN.
TO MAKE SURE A DAY LIKE THAT NEVER HAPPENS AGAIN.

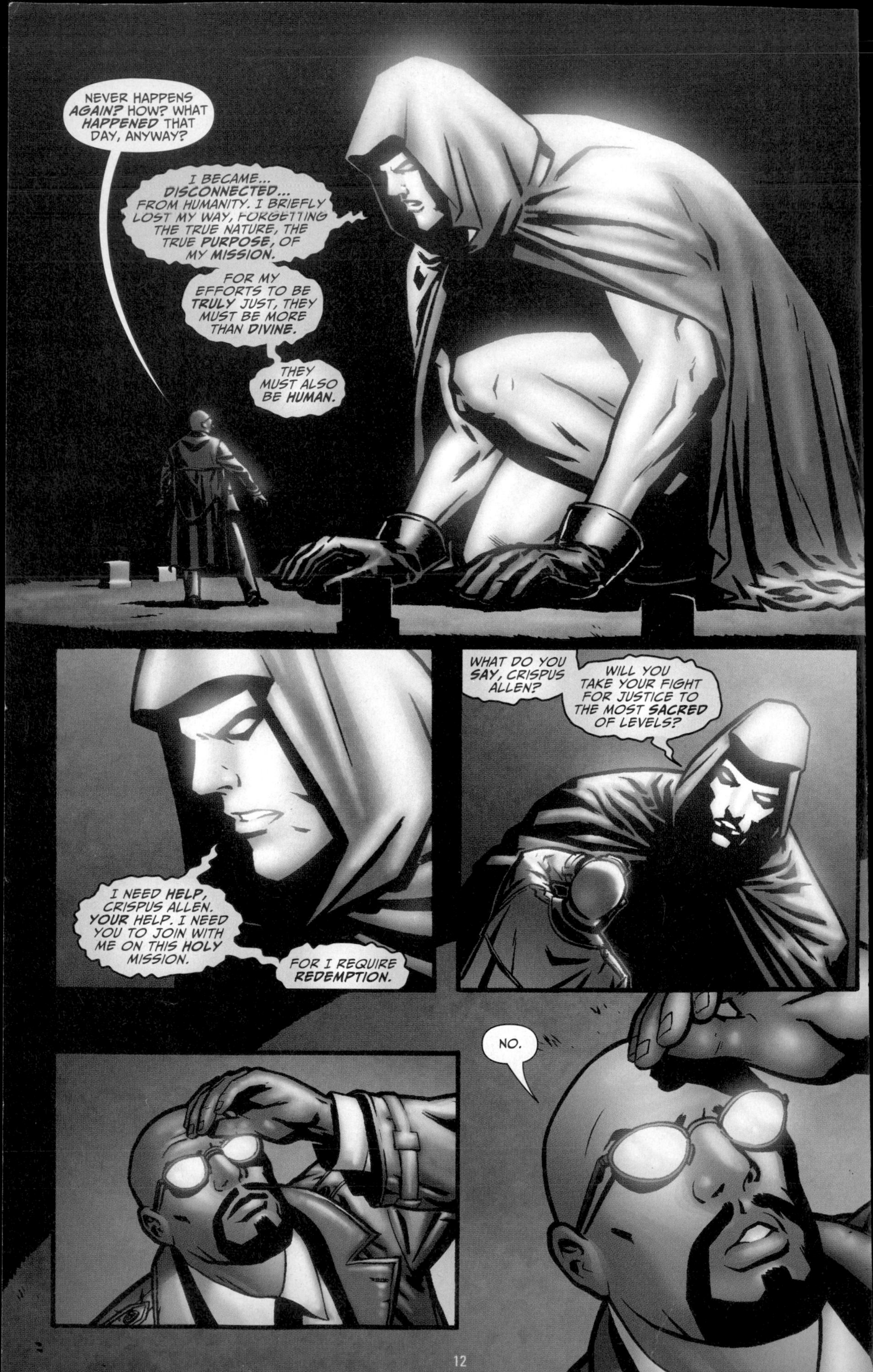
NEVER HAPPENS AGAIN? HOW? WHAT HAPPENED THAT DAY, ANYWAY?
I BECAME... DISCONNECTED... FROM HUMANITY. I BRIEFLY LOST MY WAY, FORGETTING THE TRUE NATURE, THE TRUE PURPOSE, OF MY MISSION.
FOR MY EFFORTS TO BE TRULY JUST, THEY MUST BE MORE THAN DIVINE.
THEY MUST ALSO BE HUMAN.
I NEED HELP, CRISPUS ALLEN. YOUR HELP. I NEED YOU TO JOIN WITH ME ON THIS HOLY MISSION.
FOR I REQUIRE REDEMPTION.
WHAT DO YOU SAY, CRISPUS ALLEN?
WILL YOU TAKE YOUR FIGHT FOR JUSTICE TO THE MOST SACRED OF LEVELS?
NO.

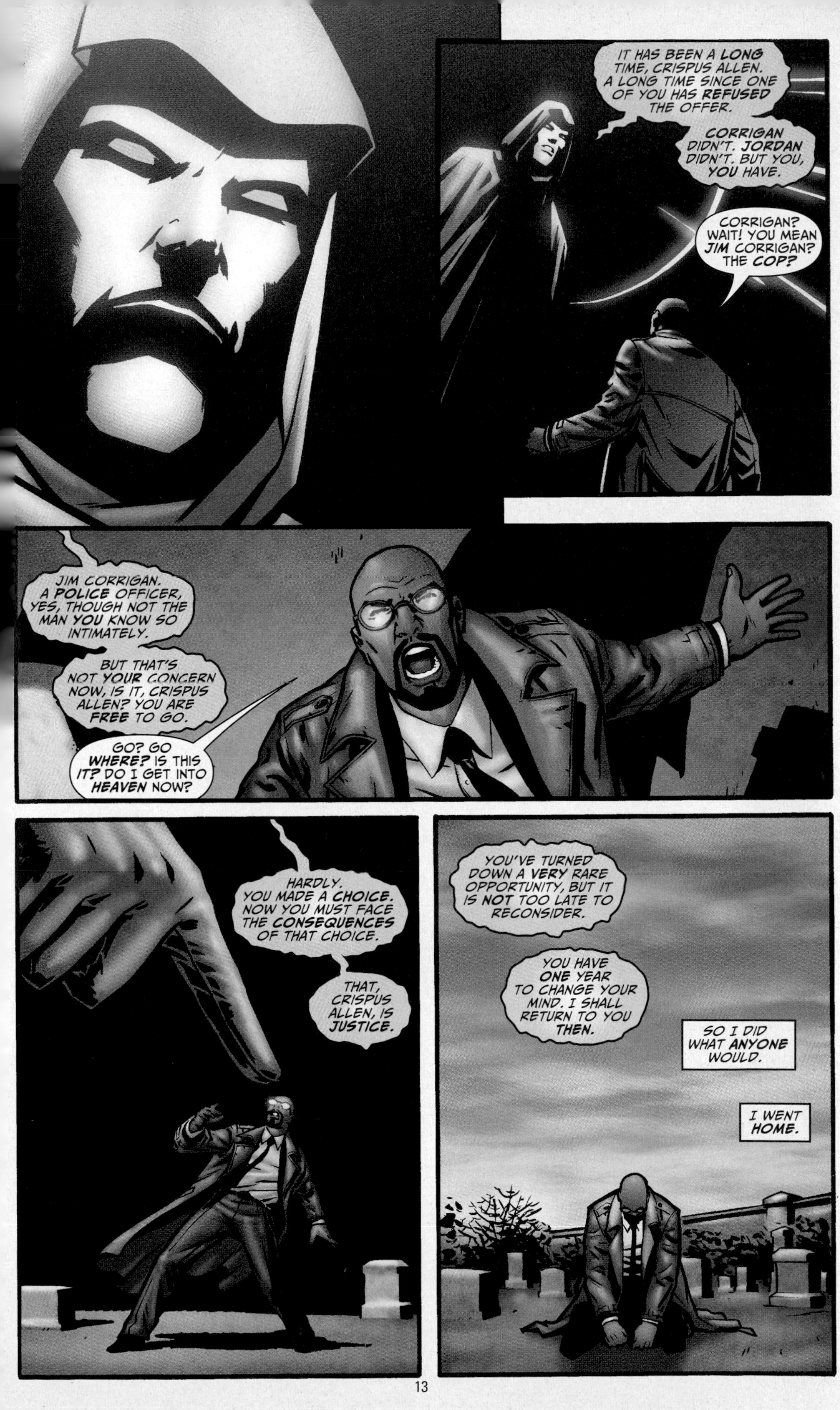
IT HAS BEEN A LONG TIME, CRISPUS ALLEN. A LONG TIME SINCE ONE OF YOU HAS REFUSED THE OFFER.
CORRIGAN DIDN'T. JORDAN DIDN'T. BUT YOU, YOU HAVE.
CORRIGAN? WAIT! YOU MEAN JIM CORRIGAN? THE COP?
JIM CORRIGAN. A POLICE OFFICER, YES, THOUGH NOT THE MAN YOU KNOW SO INTIMATELY.
BUT THAT'S NOT YOUR CONCERN NOW, IS IT, CRISPUS ALLEN? YOU ARE FREE TO GO.
GO? GO WHERE? IS THIS IT? DO I GET INTO HEAVEN NOW?
HARDLY. YOU MADE A CHOICE. NOW YOU MUST FACE THE CONSEQUENCES OF THAT CHOICE.
THAT, CRISPUS ALLEN, IS JUSTICE.
YOU'VE TURNED DOWN A VERY RARE OPPORTUNITY, BUT IT IS NOT TOO LATE TO RECONSIDER.
YOU HAVE ONE YEAR TO CHANGE YOUR MIND. I SHALL RETURN TO YOU THEN.
SO I DID WHAT ANYONE WOULD.
I WENT HOME.

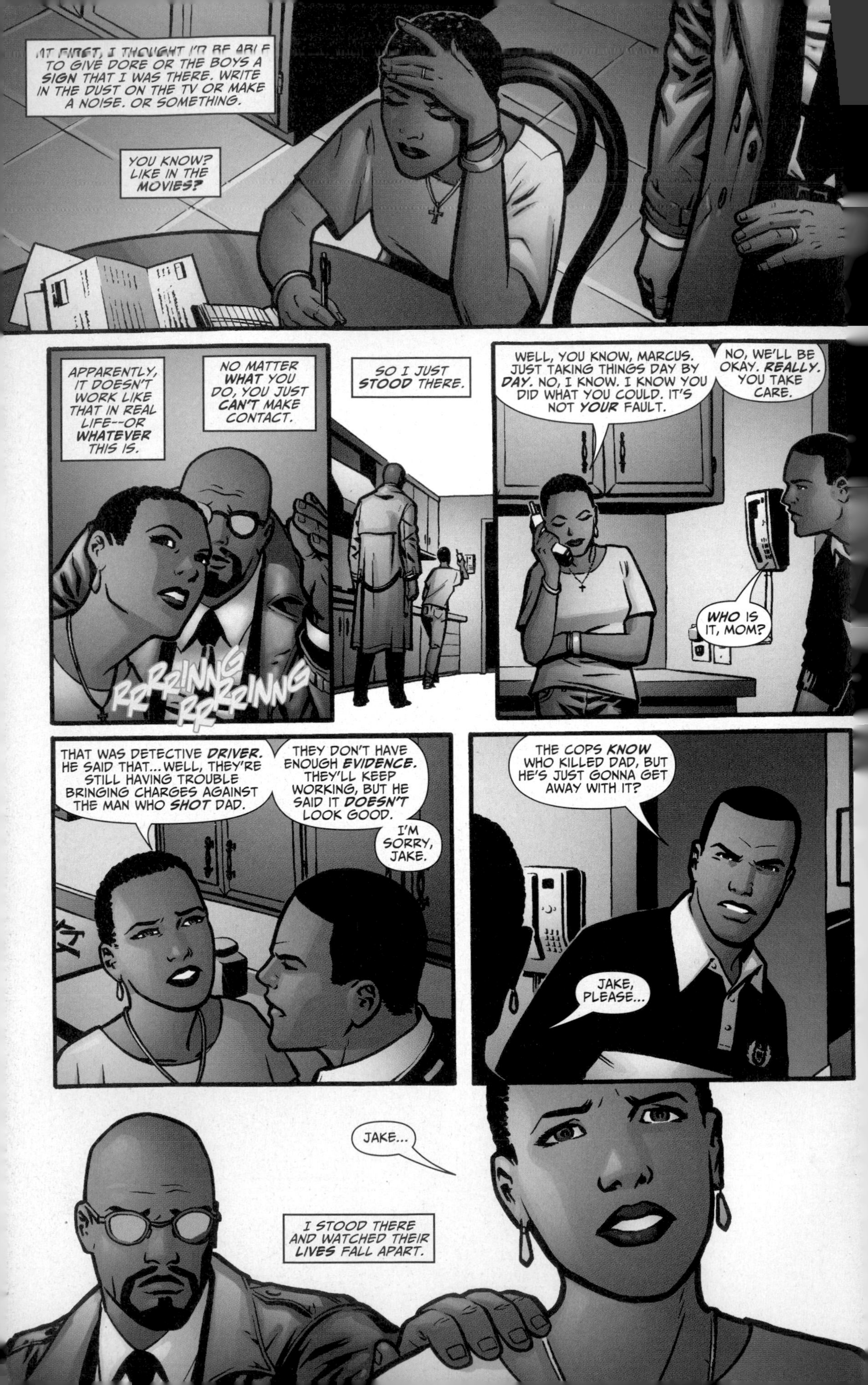
AT FIRST, I THOUGHT I'D BE ABLE TO GIVE DORE OR THE BOYS A SIGN THAT I WAS THERE. WRITE IN THE DUST ON THE TV OR MAKE A NOISE. OR SOMETHING.
YOU KNOW? LIKE IN THE MOVIES?
APPARENTLY, IT DOESN'T WORK LIKE THAT IN REAL LIFE--OR WHATEVER THIS IS.
NO MATTER WHAT YOU DO, YOU JUST CAN'T MAKE CONTACT.
RRRRINNG RRRRINNG
SO I JUST STOOD THERE.
WELL, YOU KNOW, MARCUS. JUST TAKING THINGS DAY BY DAY. NO, I KNOW. I KNOW YOU DID WHAT YOU COULD. IT'S NOT YOUR FAULT.
NO, WE'LL BE OKAY. REALLY. YOU TAKE CARE.
WHO IS IT, MOM?
THAT WAS DETECTIVE DRIVER. HE SAID THAT...WELL, THEY'RE STILL HAVING TROUBLE BRINGING CHARGES AGAINST THE MAN WHO SHOT DAD.
THEY DON'T HAVE ENOUGH EVIDENCE. THEY'LL KEEP WORKING, BUT HE SAID IT DOESN'T LOOK GOOD.
I'M SORRY, JAKE.
THE COPS KNOW WHO KILLED DAD, BUT HE'S JUST GONNA GET AWAY WITH IT?
JAKE, PLEASE...
JAKE...
I STOOD THERE AND WATCHED THEIR LIVES FALL APART.

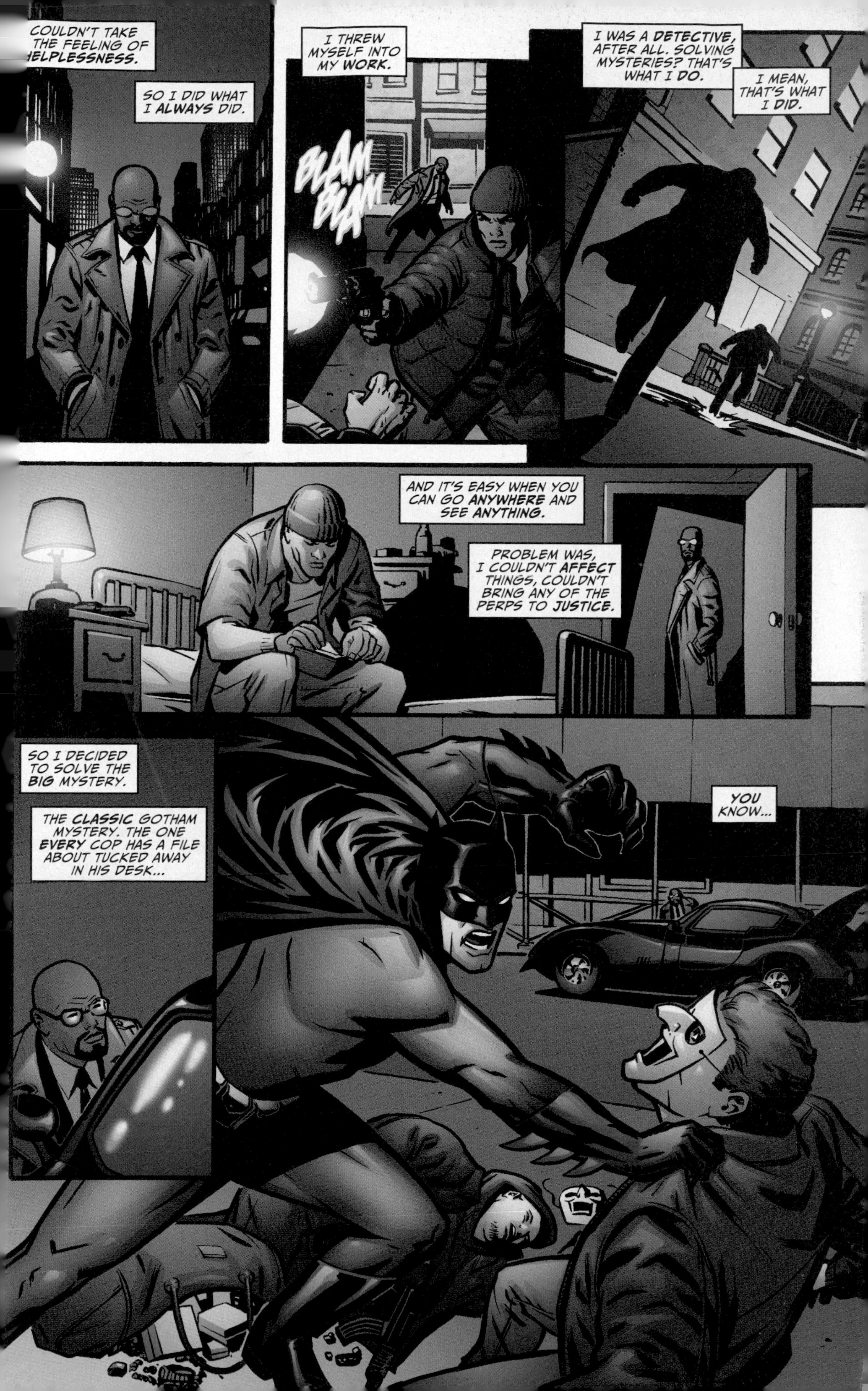

COULDN'T TAKE THE FEELING OF HELPLESSNESS.
SO I DID WHAT I ALWAYS DID.
I THREW MYSELF INTO MY WORK.
BLAM BLAM BLAM
I WAS A DETECTIVE, AFTER ALL. SOLVING MYSTERIES? THAT'S WHAT I DO.
I MEAN, THAT'S WHAT I DID.
AND IT'S EASY WHEN YOU CAN GO ANYWHERE AND SEE ANYTHING.
PROBLEM WAS, I COULDN'T AFFECT THINGS, COULDN'T BRING ANY OF THE PERPS TO JUSTICE.
SO I DECIDED TO SOLVE THE BIG MYSTERY.
THE CLASSIC GOTHAM MYSTERY. THE ONE EVERY COP HAS A FILE ABOUT TUCKED AWAY IN HIS DESK...
YOU KNOW...

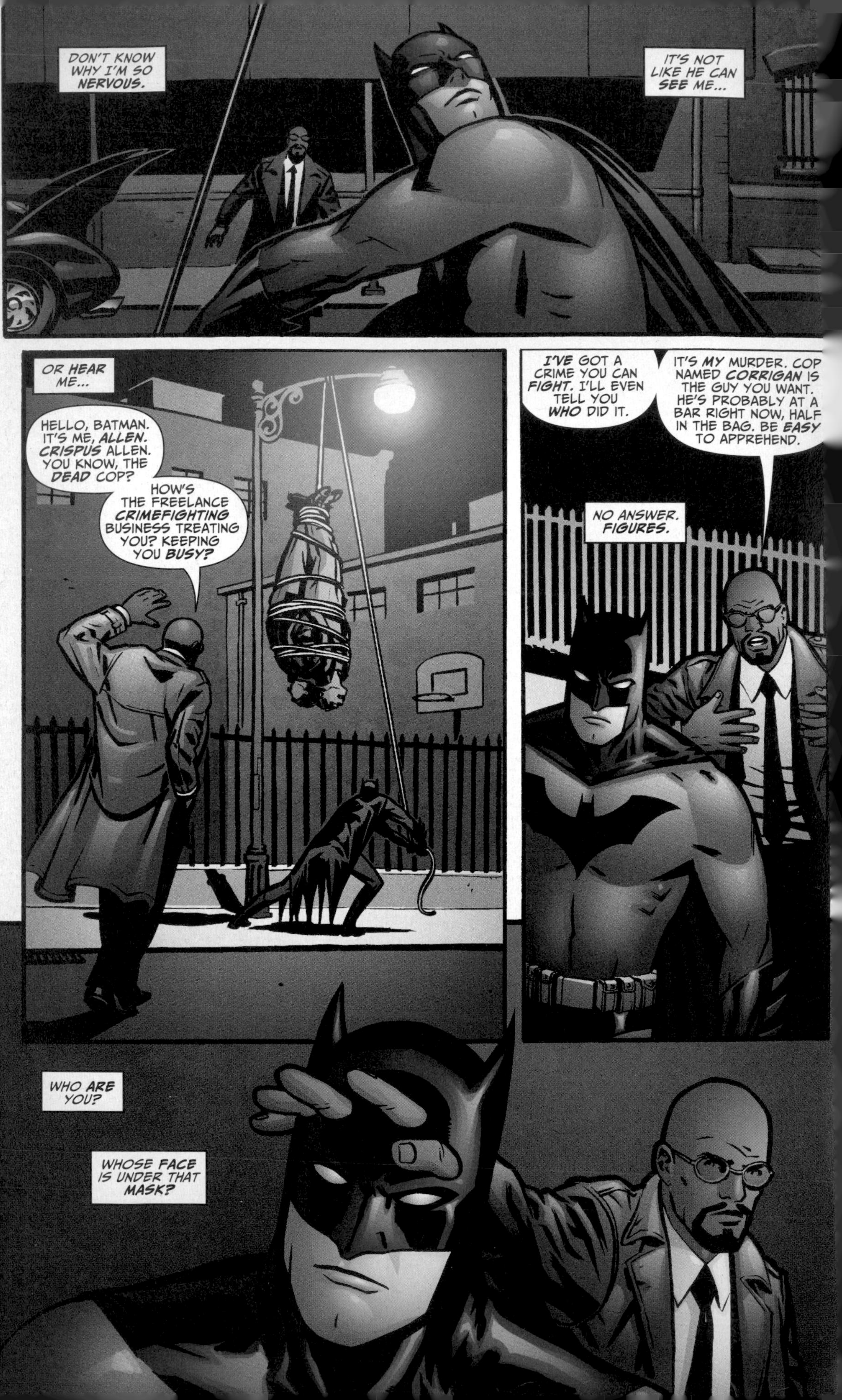
DON'T KNOW WHY I'M SO NERVOUS.
IT'S NOT LIKE HE CAN SEE ME...
OR HEAR ME...
HELLO, BATMAN. IT'S ME, ALLEN. CRISPUS ALLEN. YOU KNOW, THE DEAD COP?
HOW'S THE FREELANCE CRIMEFIGHTING BUSINESS TREATING YOU? KEEPING YOU BUSY?
I'VE GOT A CRIME YOU CAN FIGHT. I'LL EVEN TELL YOU WHO DID IT.
IT'S MY MURDER. COP NAMED CORRIGAN IS THE GUY YOU WANT. HE'S PROBABLY AT A BAR RIGHT NOW, HALF IN THE BAG. BE EASY TO APPREHEND.
NO ANSWER. FIGURES.
WHO ARE YOU?
WHOSE FACE IS UNDER THAT MASK?

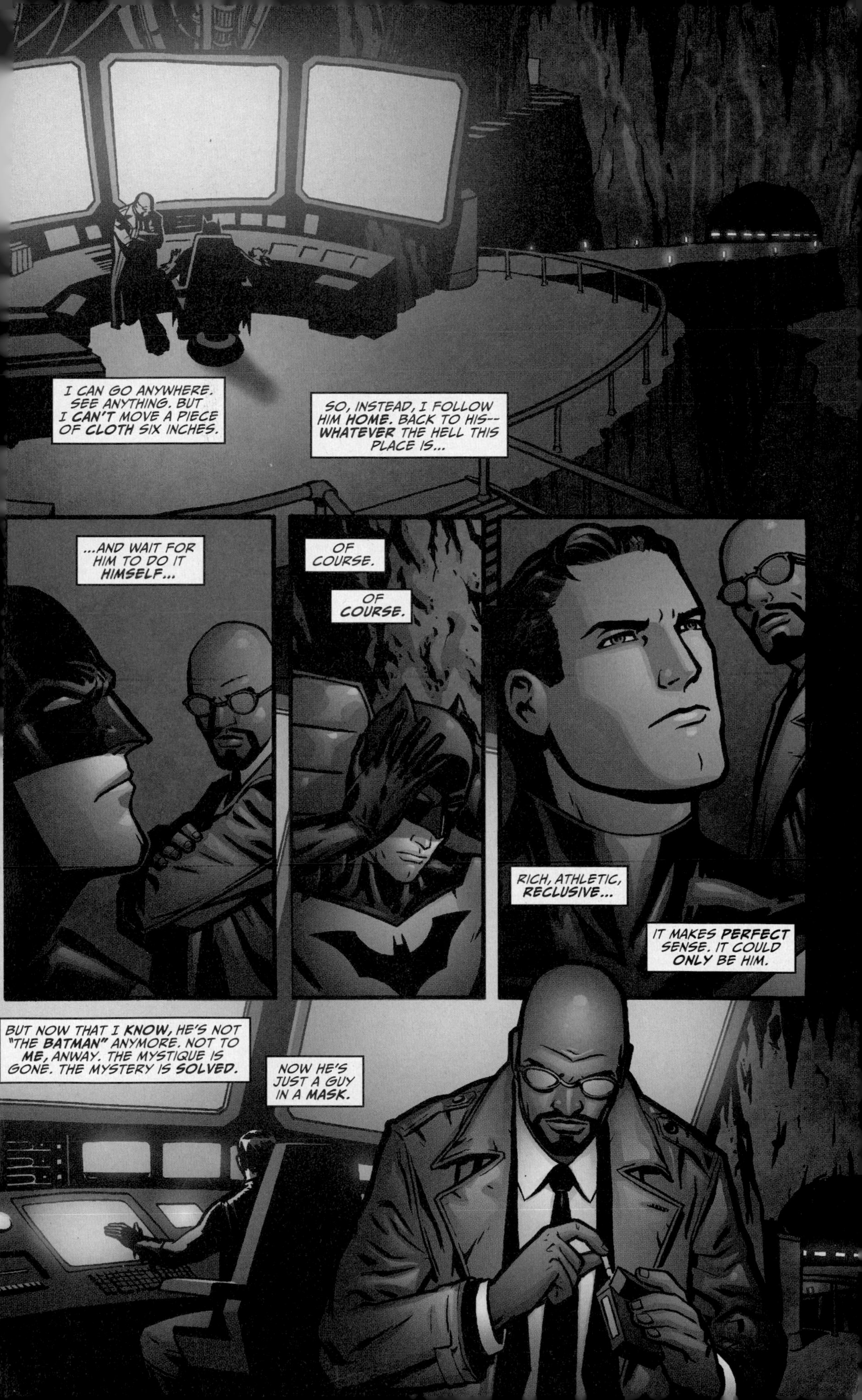
I CAN GO ANYWHERE. SEE ANYTHING. BUT I CAN'T MOVE A PIECE OF CLOTH SIX INCHES.
SO, INSTEAD, I FOLLOW HIM HOME. BACK TO HIS-- WHATEVER THE HELL THIS PLACE IS...
...AND WAIT FOR HIM TO DO IT HIMSELF...
OF COURSE.
OF COURSE.
RICH, ATHLETIC, RECLUSIVE...
IT MAKES PERFECT SENSE. IT COULD ONLY BE HIM.
BUT NOW THAT I KNOW, HE'S NOT "THE BATMAN" ANYMORE. NOT TO ME, ANWAY. THE MYSTIQUE IS GONE. THE MYSTERY IS SOLVED.
NOW HE'S JUST A GUY IN A MASK.

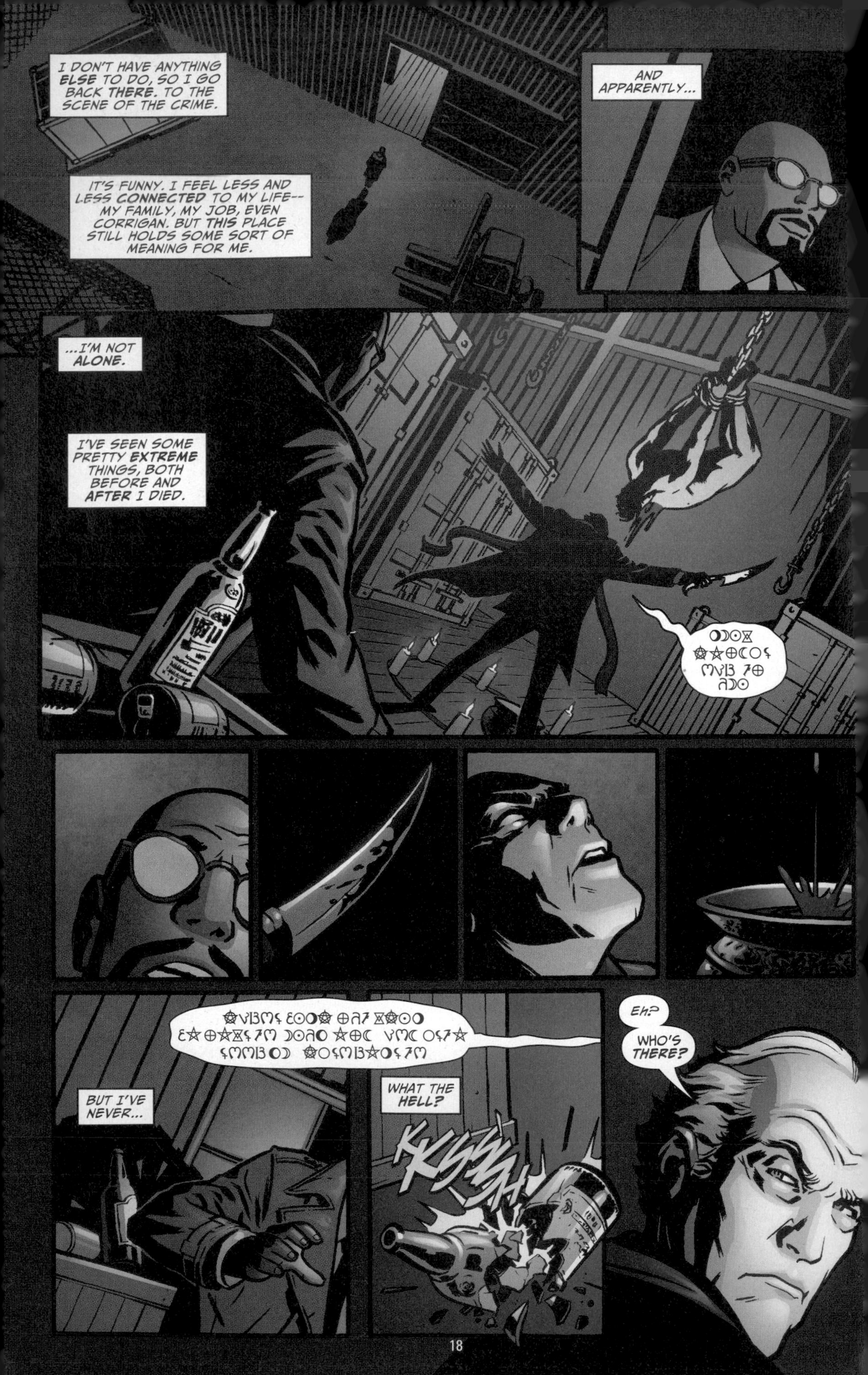
I DON'T HAVE ANYTHING ELSE TO DO, SO I GO BACK THERE. TO THE SCENE OF THE CRIME.
IT'S FUNNY. I FEEL LESS AND LESS CONNECTED TO MY LIFE-- MY FAMILY, MY JOB, EVEN CORRIGAN. BUT THIS PLACE STILL HOLDS SOME SORT OF MEANING FOR ME.
AND APPARENTLY...
...I'M NOT ALONE.
I'VE SEEN SOME PRETTY EXTREME THINGS, BOTH BEFORE AND AFTER I DIED.
BUT I'VE NEVER...
WHAT THE HELL?
KKSSH
Eh?
WHO'S THERE?

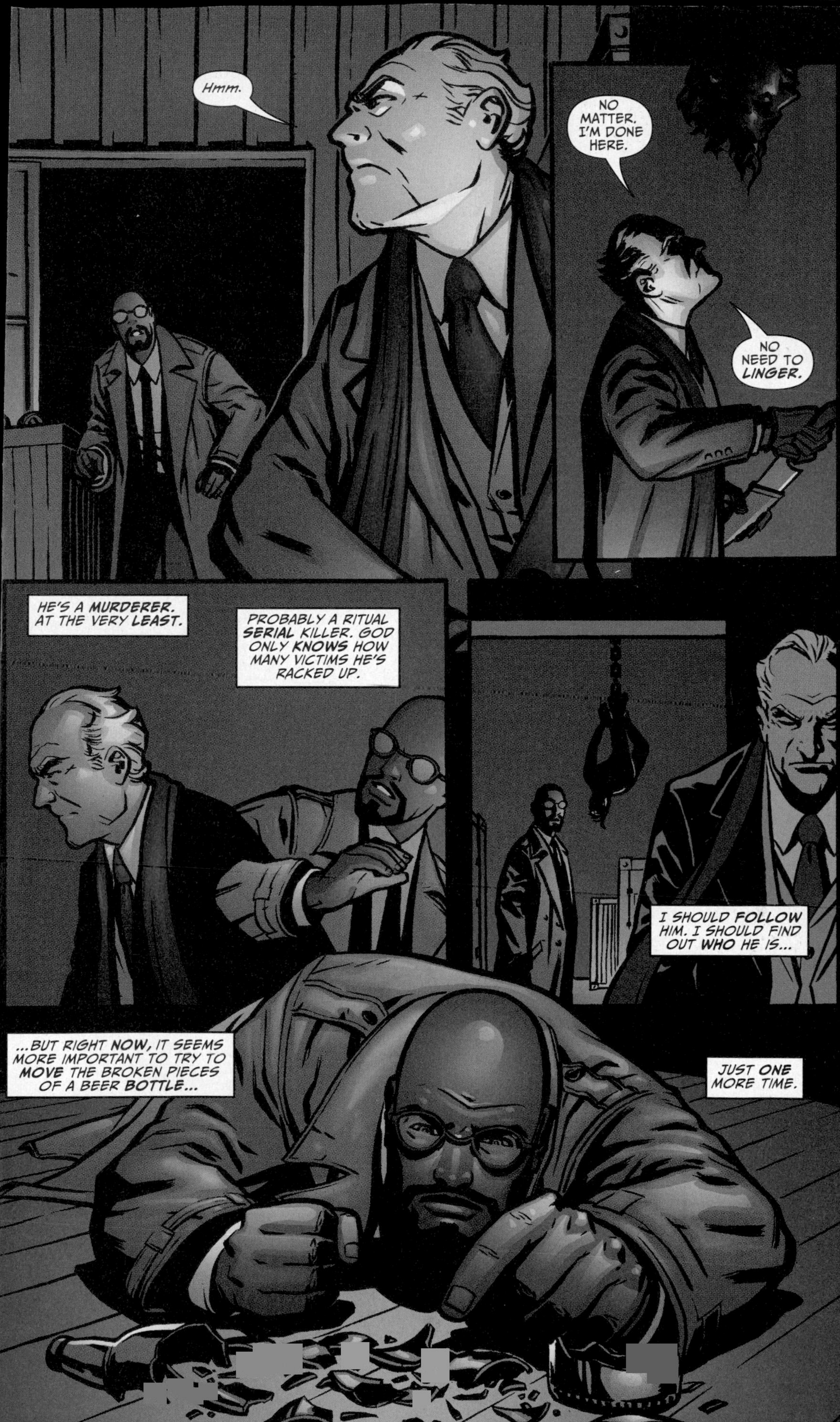
Hmm.
NO MATTER. I'M DONE HERE.
NO NEED TO LINGER.
HE'S A MURDERER. AT THE VERY LEAST.
PROBABLY A RITUAL SERIAL KILLER. GOD ONLY KNOWS HOW MANY VICTIMS HE'S RACKED UP.
I SHOULD FOLLOW HIM. I SHOULD FIND OUT WHO HE IS...
...BUT RIGHT NOW, IT SEEMS MORE IMPORTANT TO TRY TO MOVE THE BROKEN PIECES OF A BEER BOTTLE...
JUST ONE MORE TIME.

COULDN'T DO IT, THOUGH. NO MATTER HOW HARD I TRIED.

I FIGURED MAYBE IT HAD SOMETHING TO DO WITH THE KILLER, SO I CAUGHT UP WITH HIM AND STUCK LIKE GLUE. FOR WEEKS.

WARM UP YOUR COFFEE, MR. WEISS?

THANK YOU, CARLA.

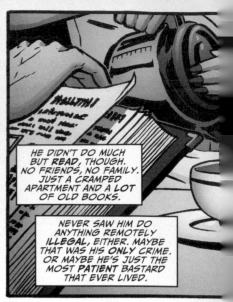

HE DIDN'T DO MUCH BUT READ, THOUGH. NO FRIENDS, NO FAMILY. JUST A CRAMPED APARTMENT AND A LOT OF OLD BOOKS.

NEVER SAW HIM DO ANYTHING REMOTELY ILLEGAL, EITHER. MAYBE THAT WAS HIS ONLY CRIME. OR MAYBE HE'S JUST THE MOST PATIENT BASTARD THAT EVER LIVED.

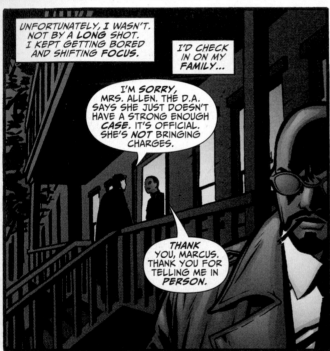

UNFORTUNATELY, I WASN'T. NOT BY A LONG SHOT. I KEPT GETTING BORED AND SHIFTING FOCUS.

I'D CHECK IN ON MY FAMILY...

I'M SORRY, MRS. ALLEN. THE D.A. SAYS SHE JUST DOESN'T HAVE A STRONG ENOUGH CASE. IT'S OFFICIAL. SHE'S NOT BRINGING CHARGES.

THANK YOU, MARCUS. THANK YOU FOR TELLING ME IN PERSON.

THEN I'D CHECK IN ON WEISS.

JUST LIKE ALWAYS, I SPLIT MY TIME BETWEEN WORK...

AND, AFTER THE BREAK, WE'LL FIND OUT WHICH CLIP WINS THE $10,000 GRAND PRIZE! YOU'VE WAITED ALL SEASON TO FIND OUT, SO DON'T MISS IT!

...AND HOME.

SO HE'S NOT GOING TO JAIL? HE'S NOT EVEN GOING TO GET ARRESTED?

NO, MAL. BUT HE'LL PAY EVENTUALLY. HE WILL.

WHOEVER DID THIS, HONEY, WHOEVER DID THIS TO DAD...

WELL, SOMEDAY, HE'S GOING TO HAVE TO ANSWER TO GOD.

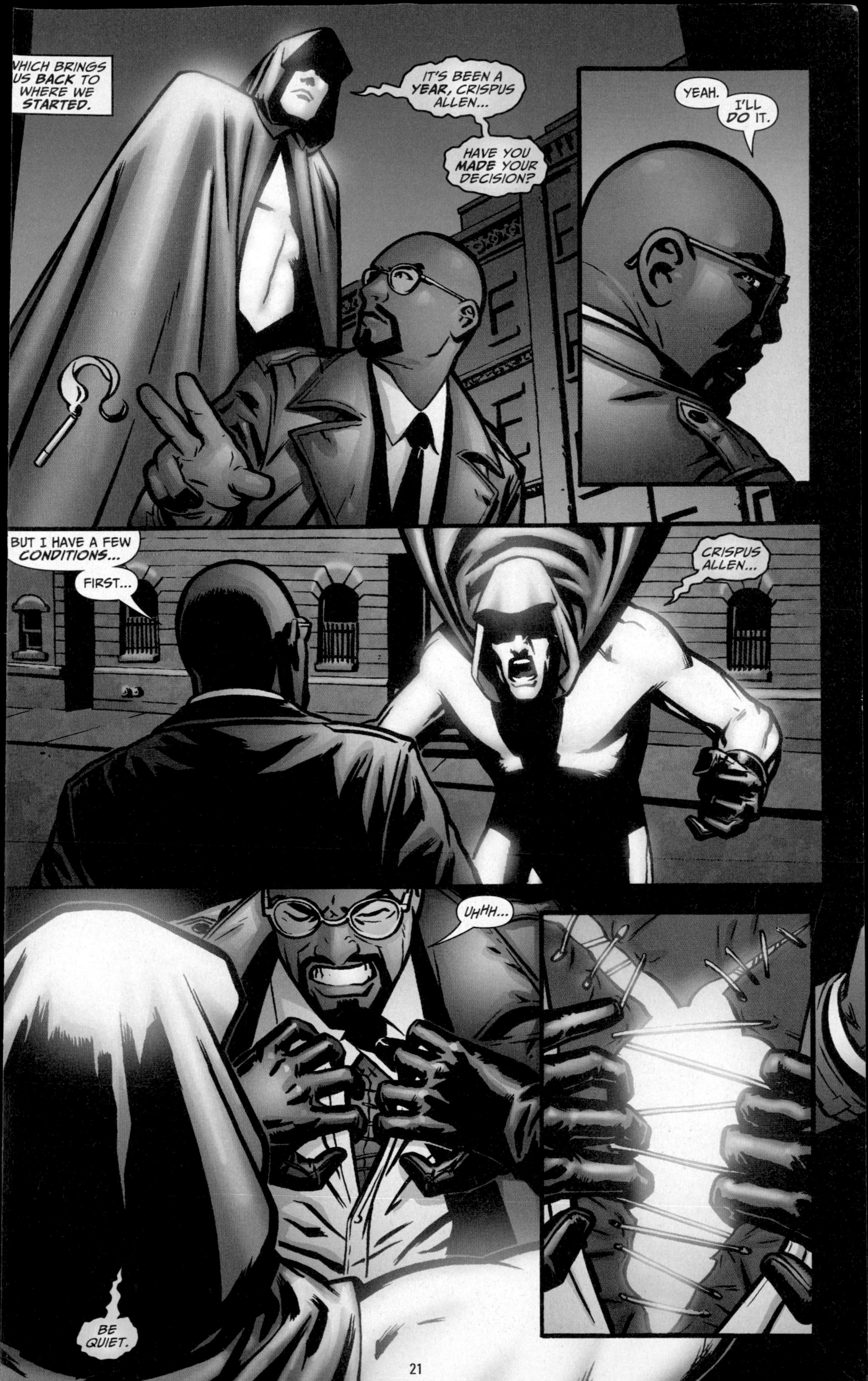
WHICH BRINGS US BACK TO WHERE WE STARTED.
IT'S BEEN A YEAR, CRISPUS ALLEN...
HAVE YOU MADE YOUR DECISION?
YEAH.
I'LL DO IT.
BUT I HAVE A FEW CONDITIONS...
FIRST...
CRISPUS ALLEN...
UHHH...
BE QUIET.

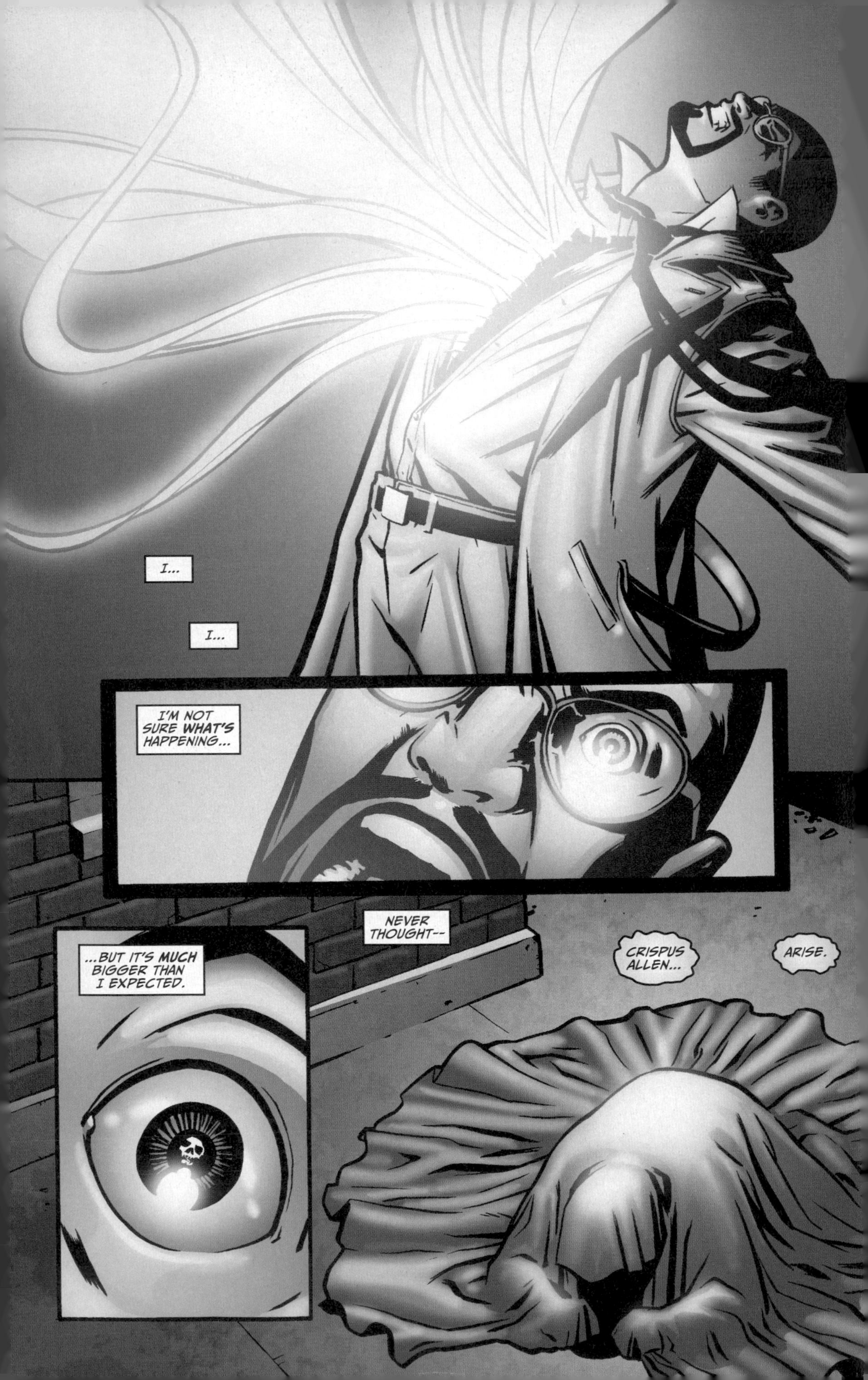
I...
I...
I'M NOT SURE WHAT'S HAPPENING...
...BUT IT'S MUCH BIGGER THAN I EXPECTED.
NEVER THOUGHT--
CRISPUS ALLEN...
ARISE.

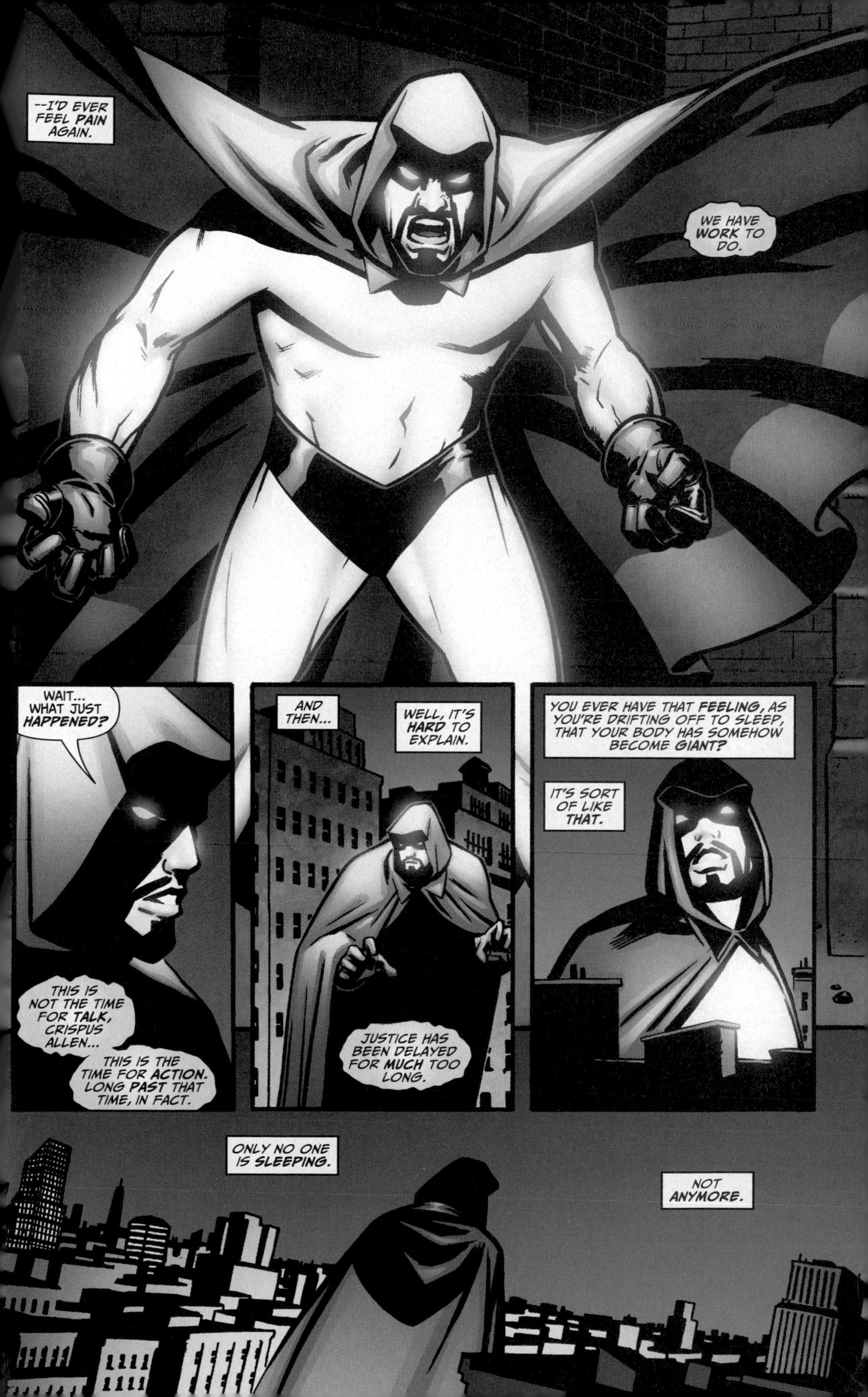
--I'D EVER FEEL PAIN AGAIN.
WE HAVE WORK TO DO.
WAIT... WHAT JUST HAPPENED?
THIS IS NOT THE TIME FOR TALK, CRISPUS ALLEN...
THIS IS THE TIME FOR ACTION. LONG PAST THAT TIME, IN FACT.
AND THEN...
WELL, IT'S HARD TO EXPLAIN.
JUSTICE HAS BEEN DELAYED FOR MUCH TOO LONG.
YOU EVER HAVE THAT FEELING, AS YOU'RE DRIFTING OFF TO SLEEP, THAT YOUR BODY HAS SOMEHOW BECOME GIANT?
IT'S SORT OF LIKE THAT.
ONLY NO ONE IS SLEEPING.
NOT ANYMORE.

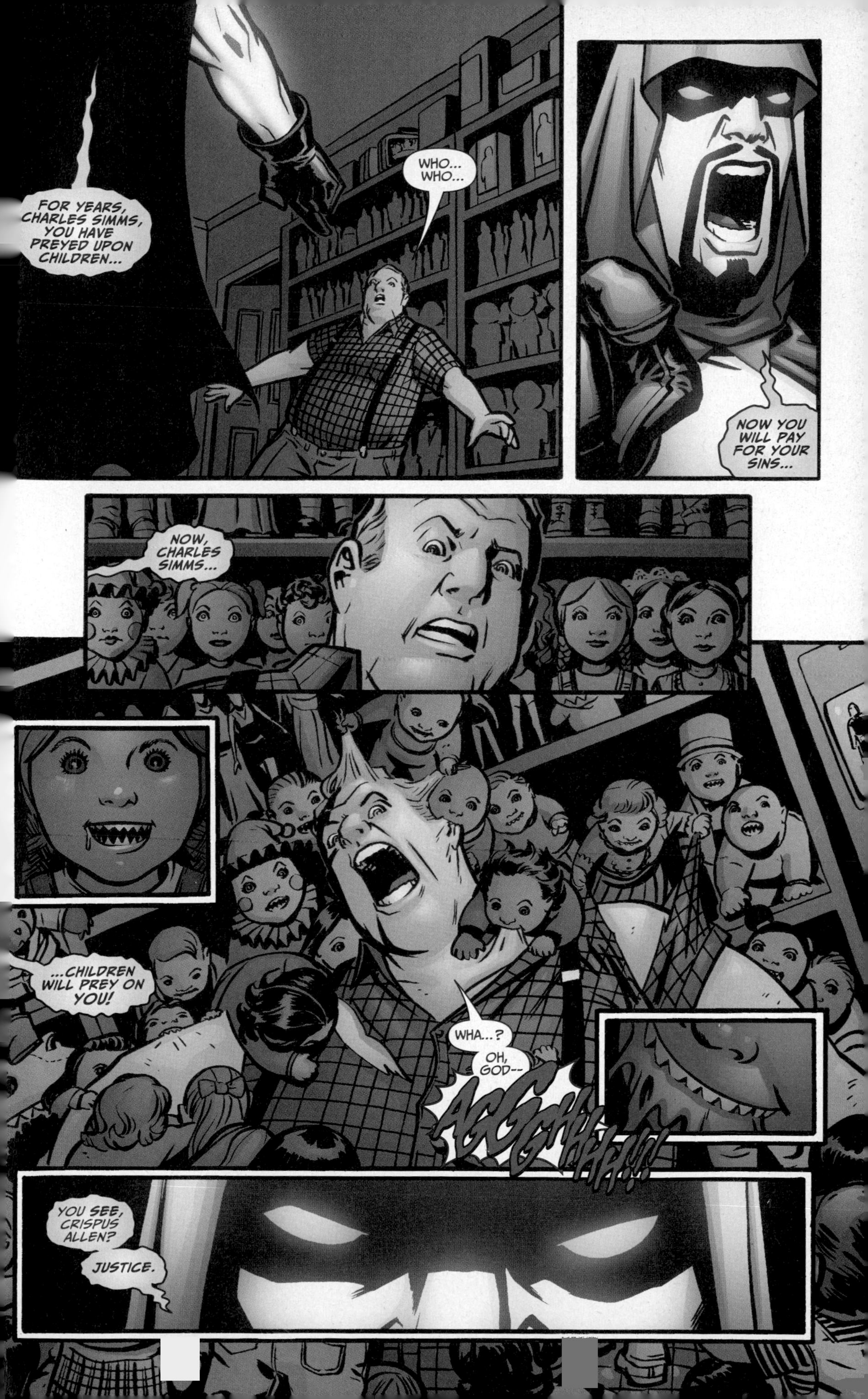
FOR YEARS, CHARLES SIMMS, YOU HAVE PREYED UPON CHILDREN...
WHO... WHO...
NOW YOU WILL PAY FOR YOUR SINS...
NOW, CHARLES SIMMS...
...CHILDREN WILL PREY ON YOU!
WHA...?
OH, GOD--
AGGHHHH!!!
YOU SEE, CRISPUS ALLEN?
JUSTICE.

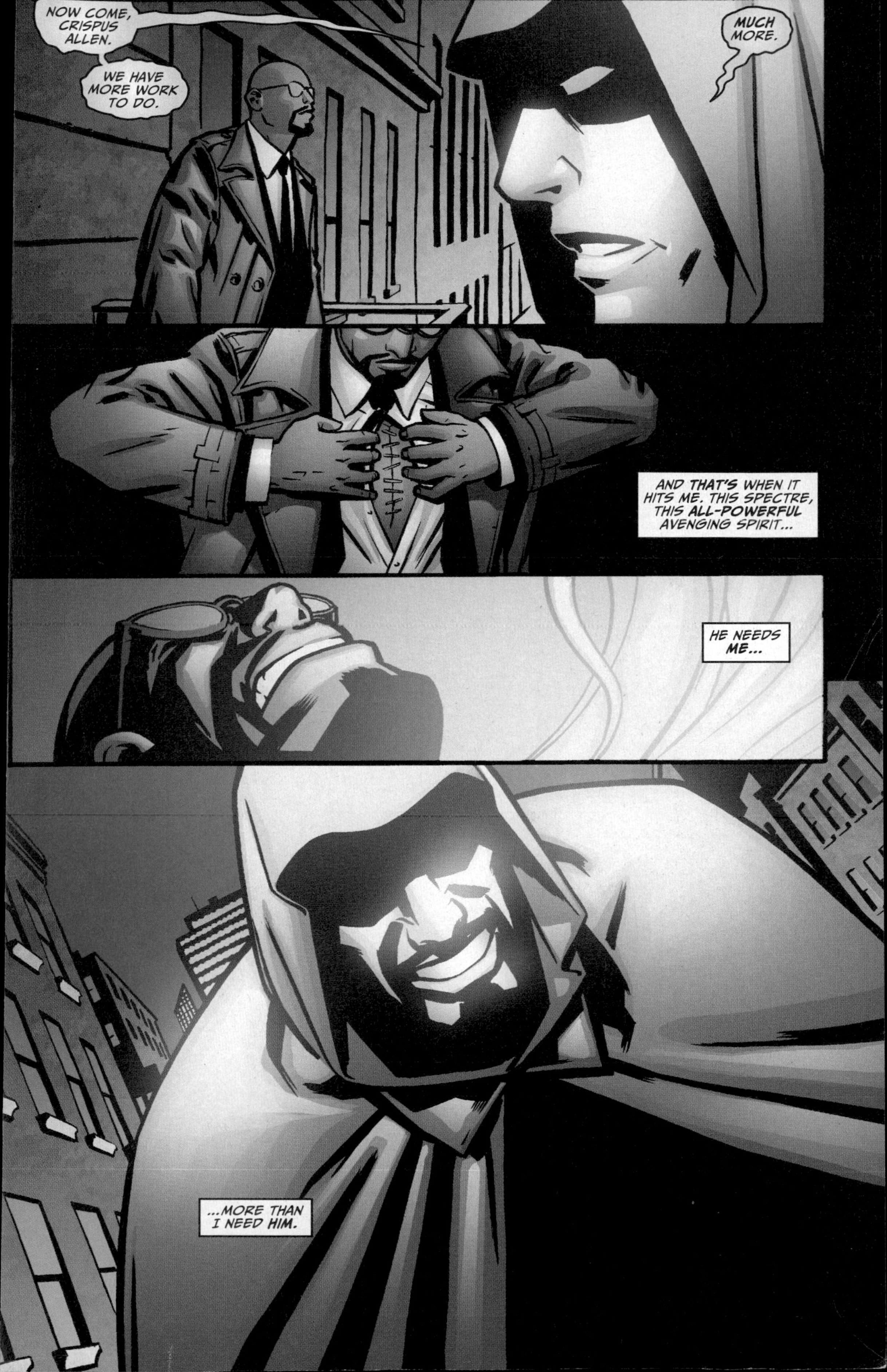
NOW COME, CRISPUS ALLEN.
WE HAVE MORE WORK TO DO.
MUCH MORE.
AND THAT'S WHEN IT HITS ME. THIS SPECTRE, THIS ALL-POWERFUL AVENGING SPIRIT...
HE NEEDS ME...
...MORE THAN I NEED HIM.

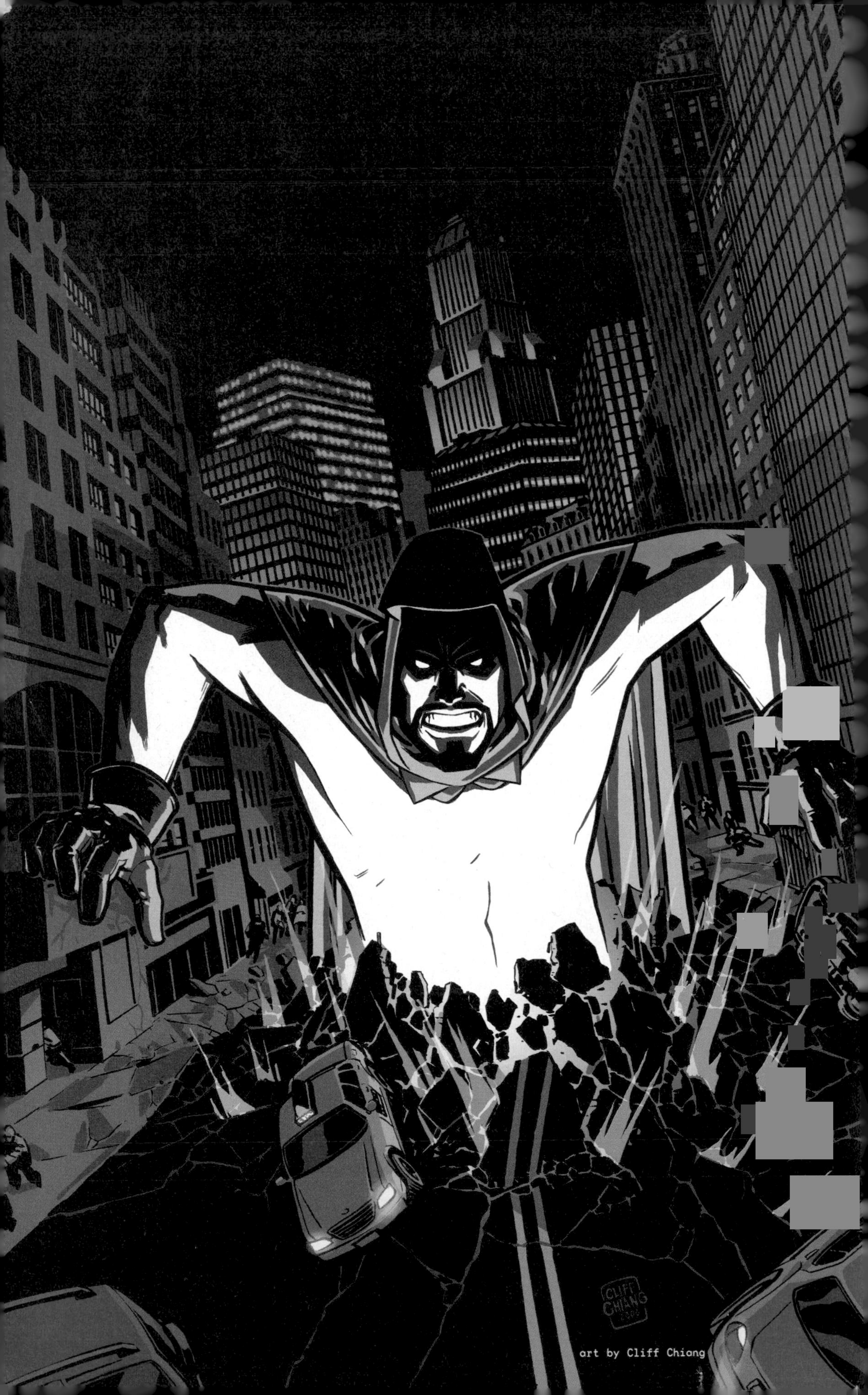
CLIFF CHIANG
art by Cliff Chiang

COPS--LIKE I WAS, NOT SO LONG AGO--WE SEE A LOT. THINGS THAT NORMAL PEOPLE-- PEOPLE LIKE YOU--NEVER SEE.

ASSAULT. RAPE. MURDER. SUICIDE. PEOPLE AT THEIR ABSOLUTE WORST. BUT HERE'S THE THING...

EVEN COPS, EVEN WITH ALL THE HORRIBLE THINGS WE SEE...WE DON'T SEE IT ALL. NOT EVEN CLOSE.

WE'RE LIKE THE CREW ON THE DECK OF THE TITANIC, STARING IN HORROR AT THE ICEBERG...

...BUT ONLY SEEING THE VERY TIP.

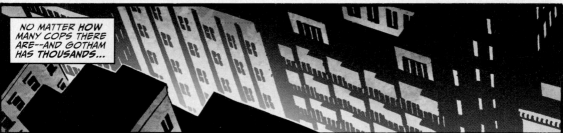

NO MATTER HOW MANY COPS THERE ARE--AND GOTHAM HAS THOUSANDS...

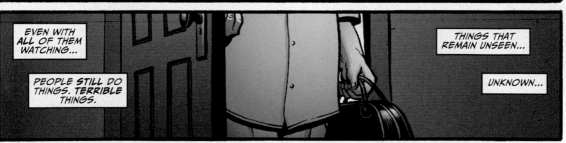

EVEN WITH ALL OF THEM WATCHING...

PEOPLE STILL DO THINGS. TERRIBLE THINGS.

THINGS THAT REMAIN UNSEEN...

UNKNOWN...

UNPUNISHED.

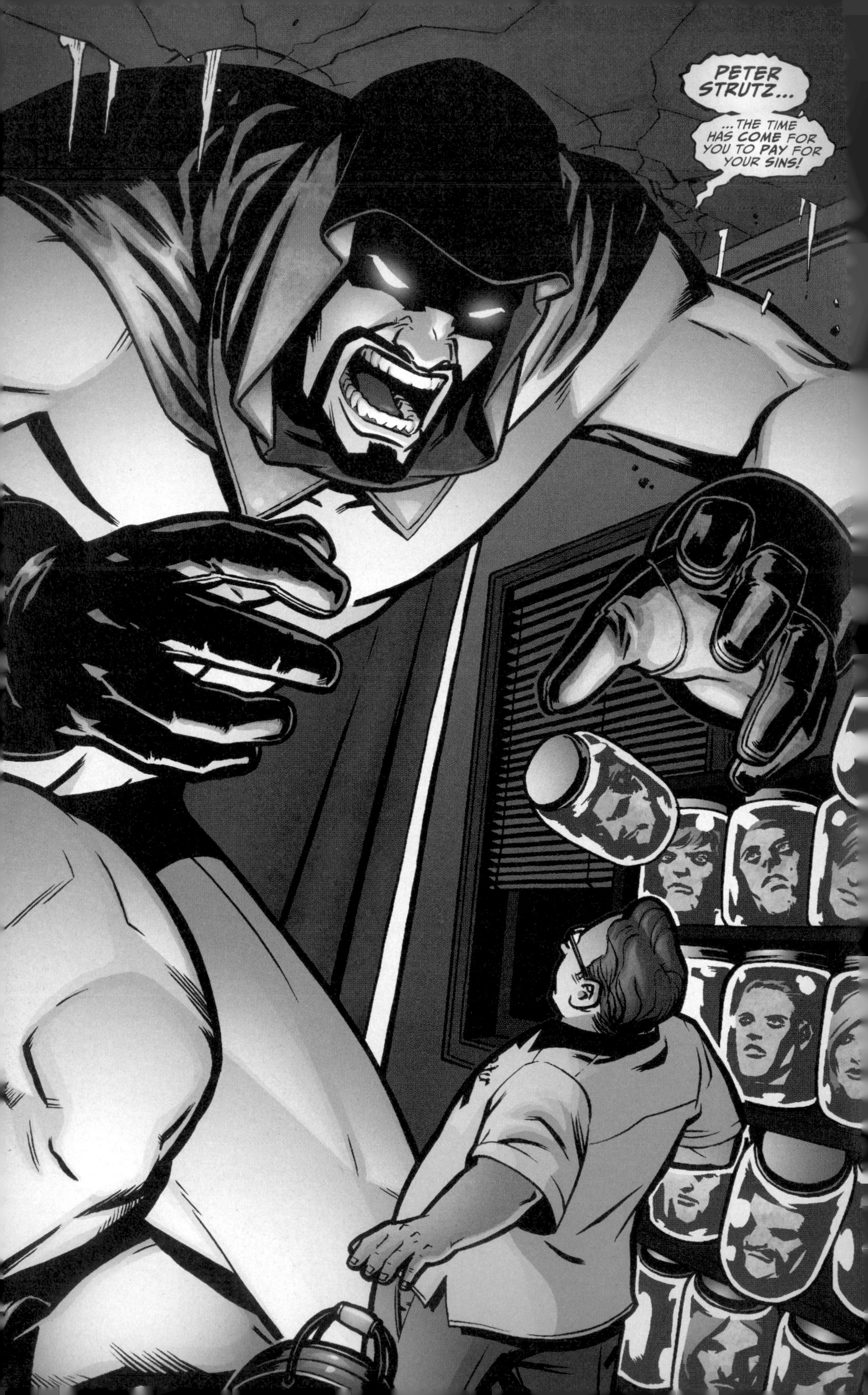
PETER STRUTZ...
...THE TIME HAS COME FOR YOU TO PAY FOR YOUR SINS!

BY NOW I'VE SEEN THIS *PLENTY* OF TIMES. I *KNOW* WHAT HE'S GOING TO DO.

WHAT *WE'RE* GOING TO DO.

I DELAYED JOINING WITH HIM FOR A *YEAR*. THAT MEANS HE WASN'T ABLE TO *PUNISH* ANYONE FOR TWELVE MONTHS. FIFTY-TWO WEEKS.

THREE-HUNDRED AND SIXTY-FIVE DAYS.

APPARENTLY, HE BUILT UP *QUITE* A BACKLOG.

BUT THAT *DOESN'T* MEAN I HAVE TO *LIKE* IT.

SKRRCH

I MEAN *WE*. *WE* BUILT UP QUITE A BACKLOG.

I'M DOING THIS WITH HIM, AFTER ALL. IN FACT, HE *CAN'T* DO IT WITHOUT ME.

31

MUCH WORK REMAINS TO BE DONE, CRISPUS ALLEN. MANY MORE MUST FACE JUDGMENT.

AS STRANGE AS MY LIFE-- OR WHATEVER THIS IS-- HAS BECOME, SOME THINGS NEVER CHANGE.

JUST LIKE BEFORE, WHEN MY PARTNER AND I ARE FINISHED FOR THE NIGHT...

...WE GO OUR SEPARATE WAYS.

LISTEN. I NEED TO TALK TO YOU. ABOUT THE WORK, I MEAN.

I UNDERSTAND WHAT WE'RE DOING. SORT OF. I MEAN, I THINK I GET IT.

BUT WHO IS IT FOR? WE KILL THE SINNERS. NO ONE ELSE CAN SEE US.

HOW DOES THIS HELP THE CAUSE OF JUSTICE?

HELP?

WHAT WE DO DOES NOT HELP THE CAUSE OF JUSTICE.

IT IS JUSTICE.

THE SUDDEN APPEARANCES, THE IRONIC DEATHS. IT'S ALL VERY IMPRESSIVE, VERY DRAMATIC, SURE.

IN THERE? AIN'T *NOBODY* LIVED THERE SINCE I BEEN HERE, AND I BEEN HERE A LONG, *LONG* TIME.

SO WHAT'S THE *COMPLAINT,* THEN? IS SOMEONE SQUATTING IN THERE? ARE THEY MAKING TOO MUCH *NOISE?*

NOISE? WHAT'S THE MATTER WITH YOU? YOU GOT NO *NOSE?* IT'S THE DAMN *SMELL* COMING OUT OF THERE! *THAT'S* WHY I CALLED!

OKAY, OKAY...*CALM* DOWN.

NOW JUST *STEP* BACK, MA'AM...

DO YOU *REMEMBER,* CRISPUS ALLEN? DO YOU REMEMBER WHAT LAY *BEHIND* THAT DOOR?

YES...

HOW COULD I *EVER* FORGET?

WAIT...

...WHILE I SEE WHAT THE *PROBLEM* IS.

DON'T OPEN THE *DOOR.*

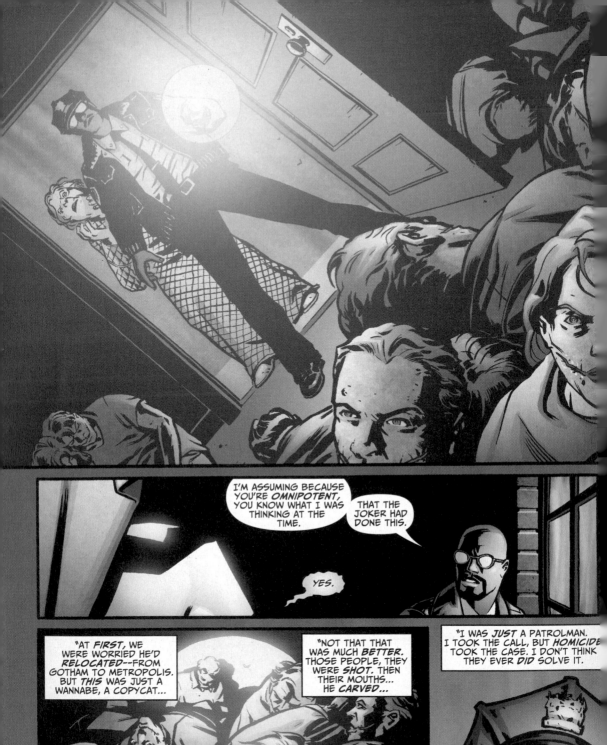

I'M ASSUMING BECAUSE YOU'RE *OMNIPOTENT*, YOU KNOW WHAT I WAS THINKING AT THE TIME.

THAT THE JOKER HAD DONE THIS.

YES.

"AT *FIRST*, WE WERE WORRIED HE'D *RELOCATED*--FROM GOTHAM TO METROPOLIS. BUT *THIS* WAS JUST A WANNABE, A COPYCAT...

"NOT THAT THAT WAS MUCH *BETTER*. THOSE PEOPLE, THEY WERE *SHOT*. THEN THEIR MOUTHS... HE *CARVED*...

"I WAS *JUST* A PATROLMAN. I TOOK THE CALL, BUT *HOMICIDE* TOOK THE CASE. I DON'T THINK THEY EVER *DID* SOLVE IT.

"IT'S AN *OLD* STORY. CRIME, BUT NO *PUNISHMENT.*

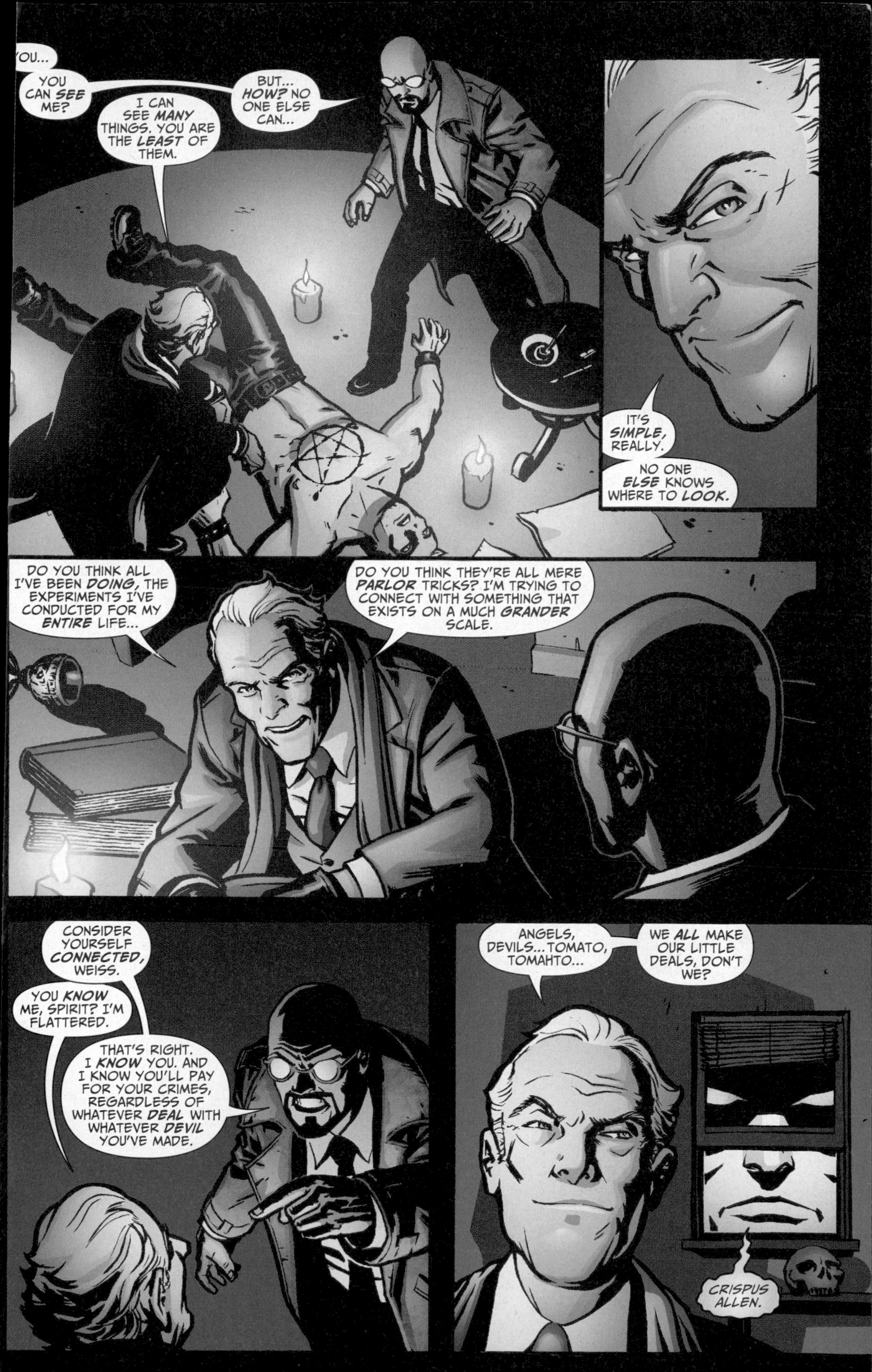
YOU...
YOU CAN *SEE* ME?
BUT... *HOW?* NO ONE ELSE CAN...
I CAN SEE *MANY* THINGS. YOU ARE THE *LEAST* OF THEM.
IT'S *SIMPLE*, REALLY.
NO ONE *ELSE* KNOWS WHERE TO *LOOK*.
DO YOU THINK ALL I'VE BEEN *DOING*, THE EXPERIMENTS I'VE CONDUCTED FOR MY *ENTIRE* LIFE...
DO YOU THINK THEY'RE ALL MERE *PARLOR* TRICKS? I'M TRYING TO CONNECT WITH SOMETHING THAT EXISTS ON A MUCH *GRANDER* SCALE.
CONSIDER YOURSELF *CONNECTED*, WEISS.
YOU *KNOW* ME, SPIRIT? I'M FLATTERED.
THAT'S RIGHT. I *KNOW* YOU. AND I KNOW YOU'LL PAY FOR YOUR CRIMES, REGARDLESS OF WHATEVER *DEAL* WITH WHATEVER *DEVIL* YOU'VE MADE.
ANGELS, DEVILS... TOMATO, TOMAHTO...
WE *ALL* MAKE OUR LITTLE DEALS, DON'T WE?
CRISPUS ALLEN.

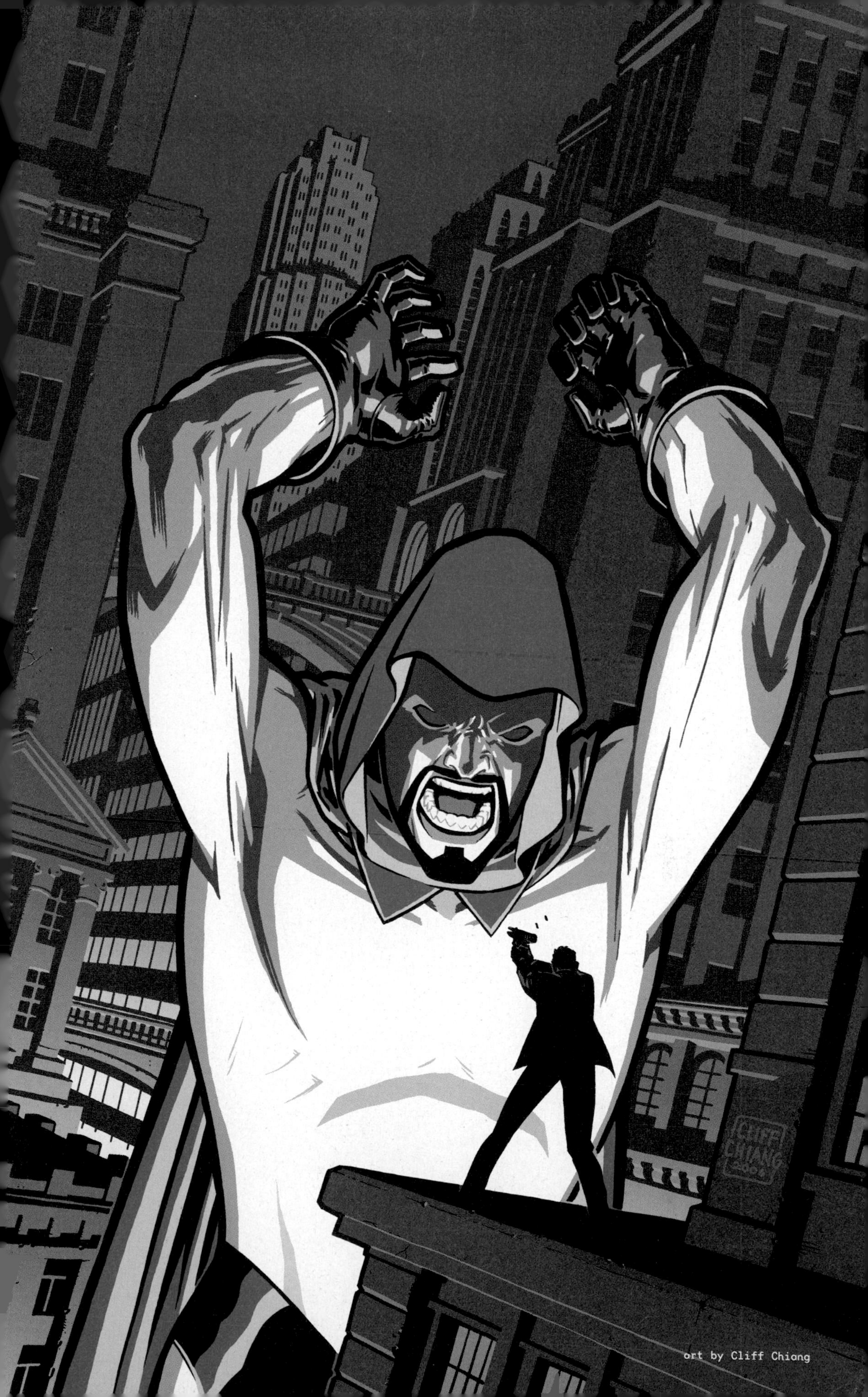
CLIFF CHIANG

art by Cliff Chiang

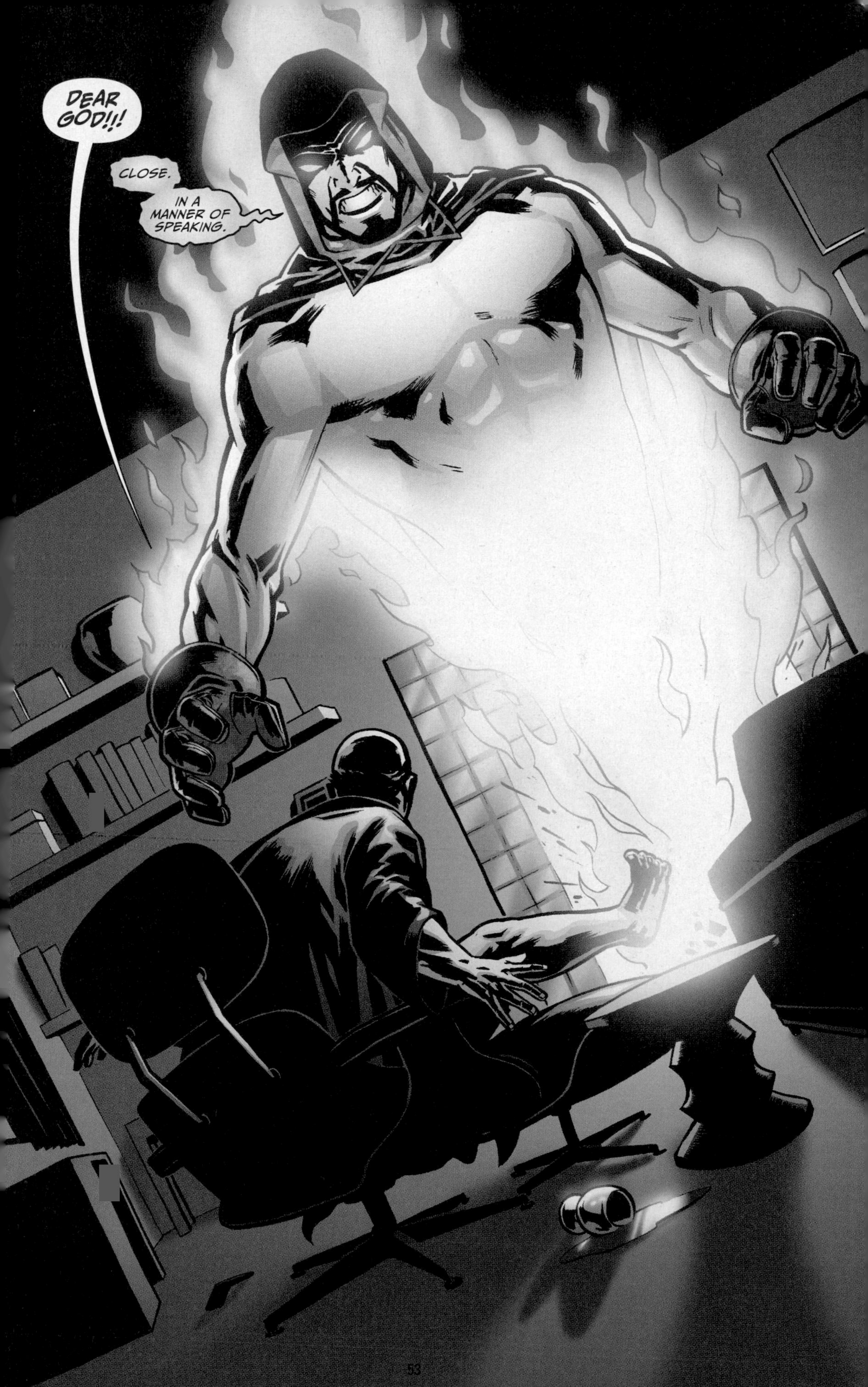
DEAR GOD!!!
CLOSE.
IN A MANNER OF SPEAKING.

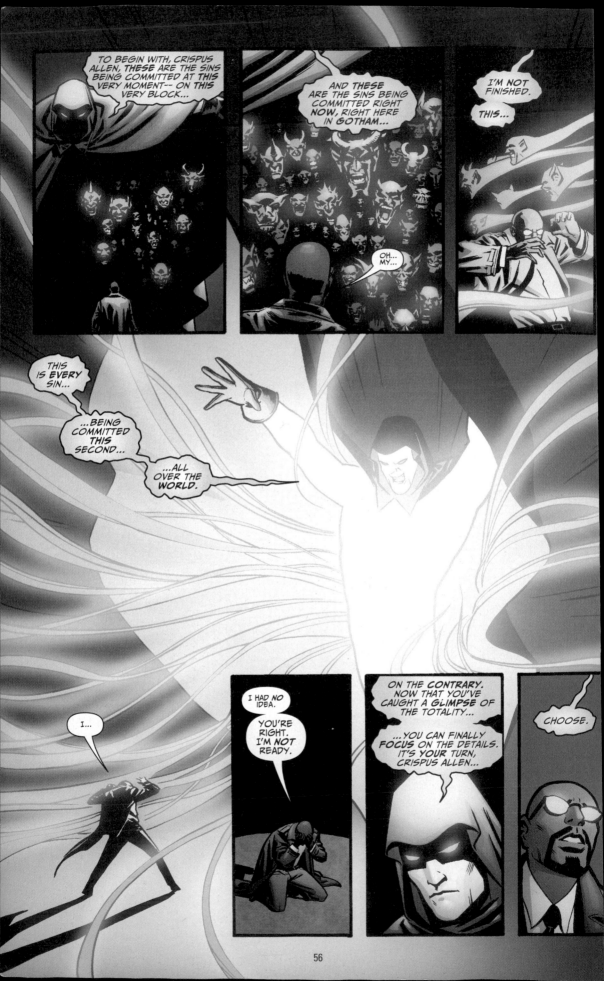

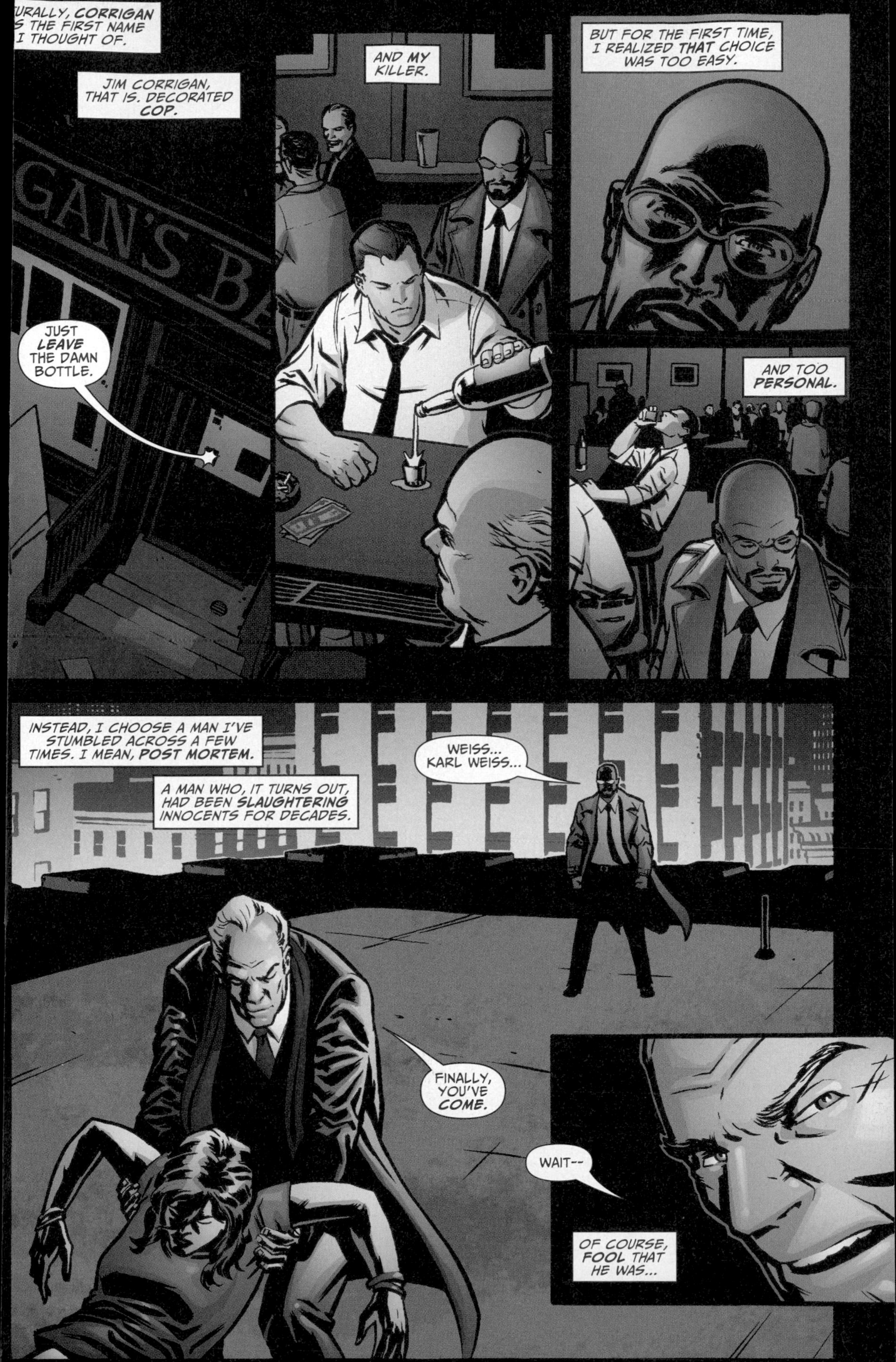
URALLY, CORRIGAN S THE FIRST NAME I THOUGHT OF.
JIM CORRIGAN, THAT IS. DECORATED COP.
GAN'S BA
JUST LEAVE THE DAMN BOTTLE.
AND MY KILLER.
BUT FOR THE FIRST TIME, I REALIZED THAT CHOICE WAS TOO EASY.
AND TOO PERSONAL.
INSTEAD, I CHOOSE A MAN I'VE STUMBLED ACROSS A FEW TIMES. I MEAN, POST MORTEM.
A MAN WHO, IT TURNS OUT, HAD BEEN SLAUGHTERING INNOCENTS FOR DECADES.
WEISS... KARL WEISS...
FINALLY, YOU'VE COME.
WAIT--
OF COURSE, FOOL THAT HE WAS...

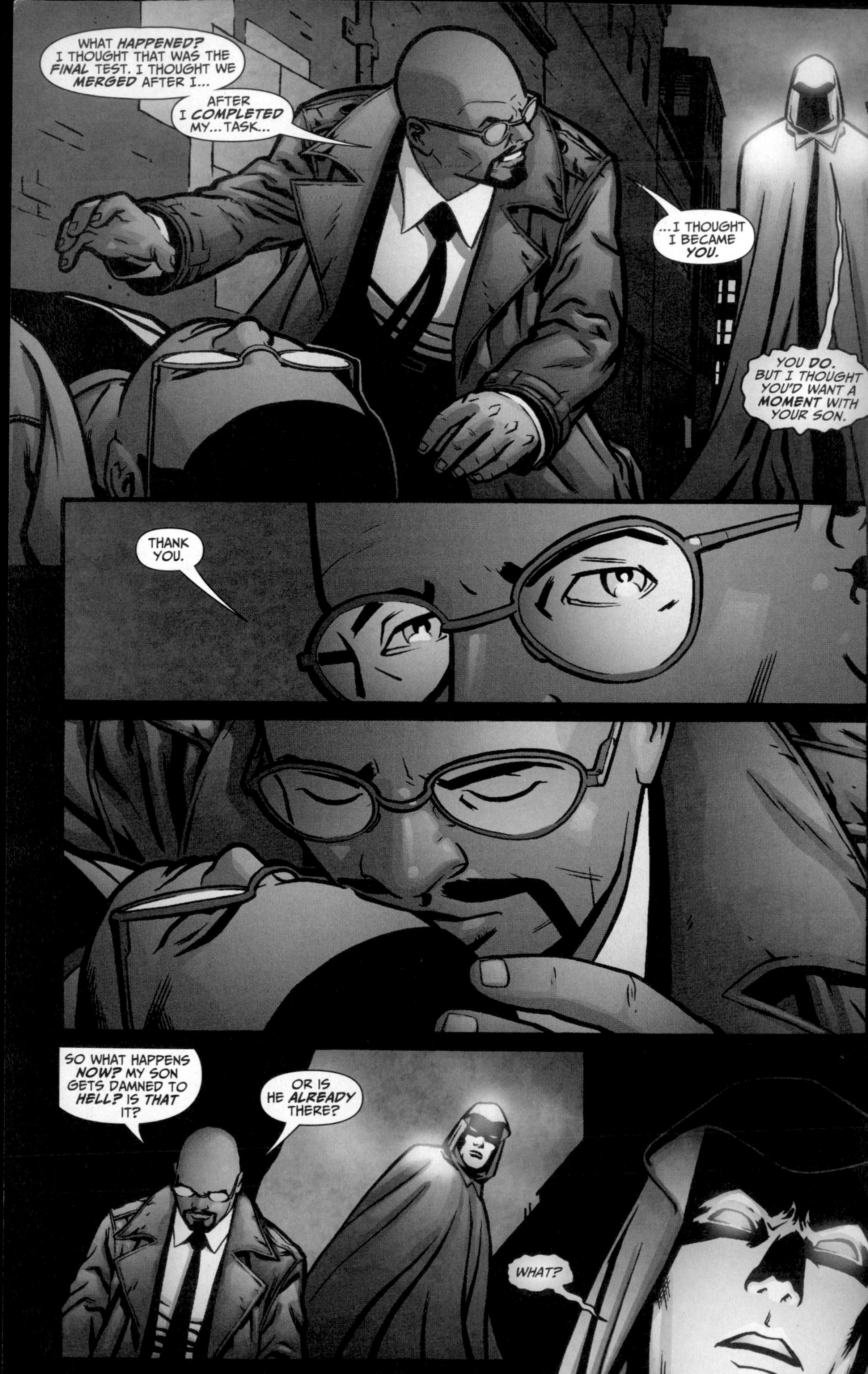
WHAT HAPPENED? I THOUGHT THAT WAS THE FINAL TEST. I THOUGHT WE MERGED AFTER I...
AFTER I COMPLETED MY... TASK...
...I THOUGHT I BECAME YOU.
YOU DO. BUT I THOUGHT YOU'D WANT A MOMENT WITH YOUR SON.
THANK YOU.
SO WHAT HAPPENS NOW? MY SON GETS DAMNED TO HELL? IS THAT IT?
OR IS HE ALREADY THERE?
WHAT?

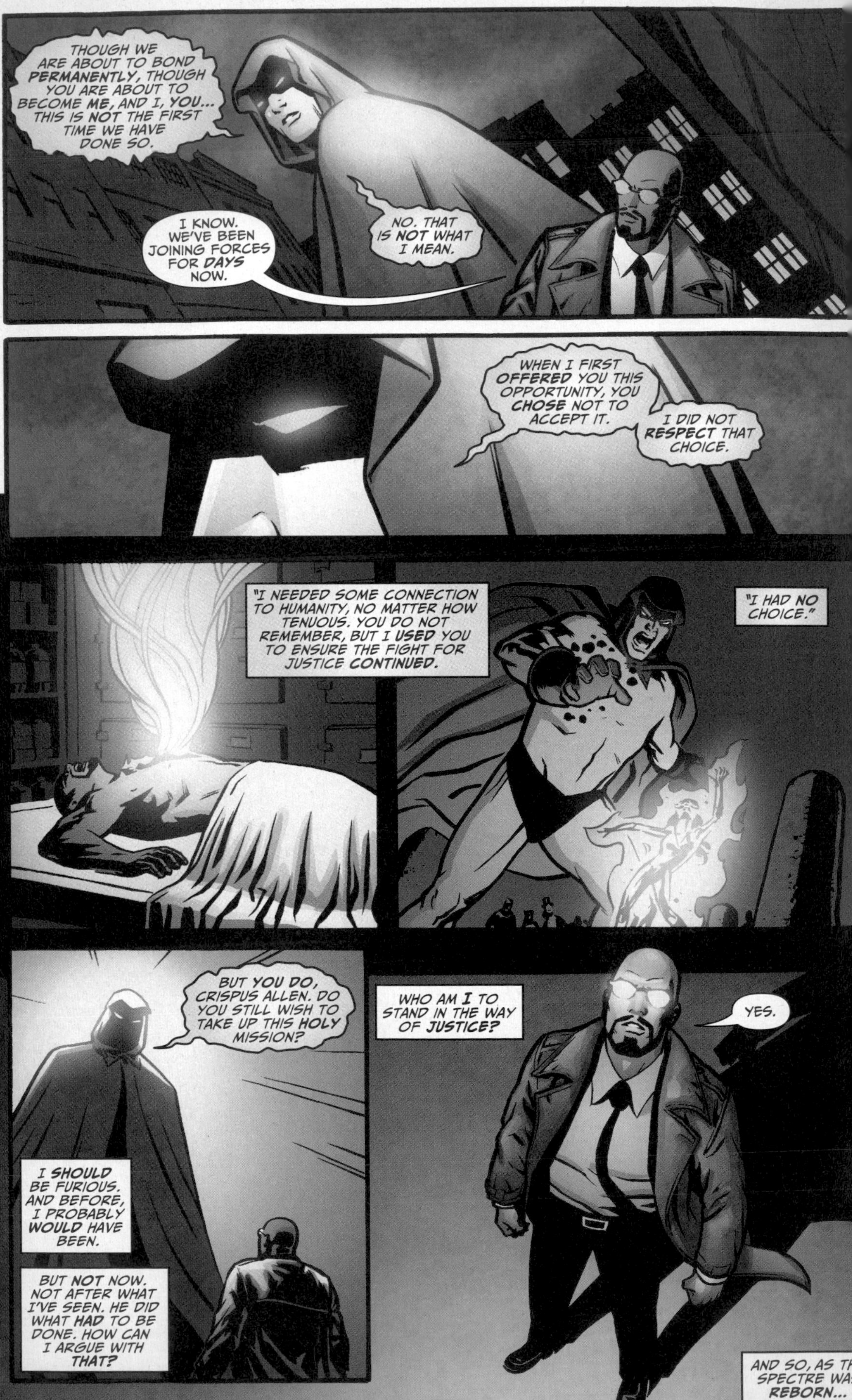
THOUGH WE ARE ABOUT TO BOND PERMANENTLY, THOUGH YOU ARE ABOUT TO BECOME ME, AND I, YOU... THIS IS NOT THE FIRST TIME WE HAVE DONE SO.
I KNOW. WE'VE BEEN JOINING FORCES FOR DAYS NOW.
NO. THAT IS NOT WHAT I MEAN.
WHEN I FIRST OFFERED YOU THIS OPPORTUNITY, YOU CHOSE NOT TO ACCEPT IT.
I DID NOT RESPECT THAT CHOICE.
"I NEEDED SOME CONNECTION TO HUMANITY, NO MATTER HOW TENUOUS. YOU DO NOT REMEMBER, BUT I USED YOU TO ENSURE THE FIGHT FOR JUSTICE CONTINUED.
"I HAD NO CHOICE."
BUT YOU DO, CRISPUS ALLEN. DO YOU STILL WISH TO TAKE UP THIS HOLY MISSION?
I SHOULD BE FURIOUS. AND BEFORE, I PROBABLY WOULD HAVE BEEN.
BUT NOT NOW. NOT AFTER WHAT I'VE SEEN. HE DID WHAT HAD TO BE DONE. HOW CAN I ARGUE WITH THAT?
WHO AM I TO STAND IN THE WAY OF JUSTICE?
YES.
AND SO, AS THE SPECTRE WAS REBORN...

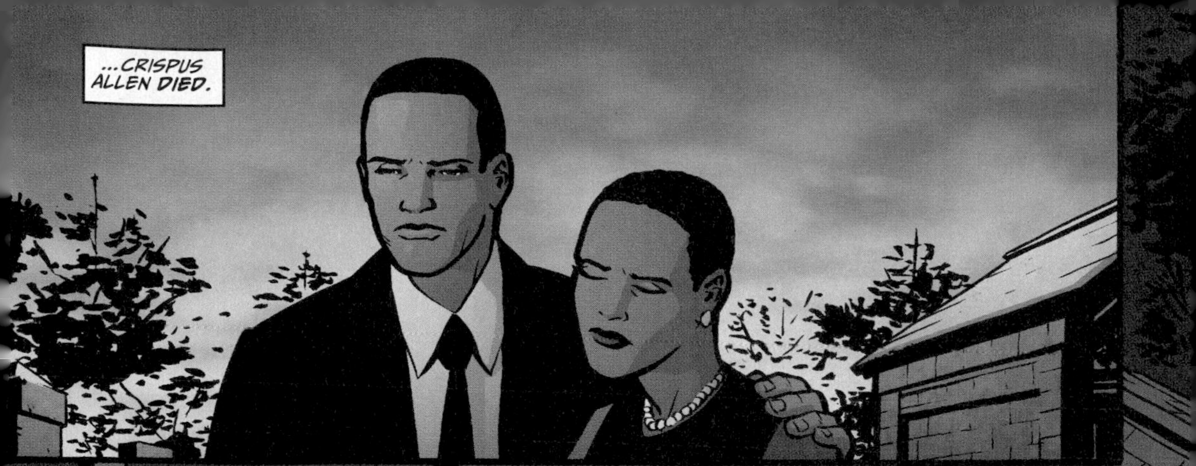
...CRISPUS ALLEN DIED.

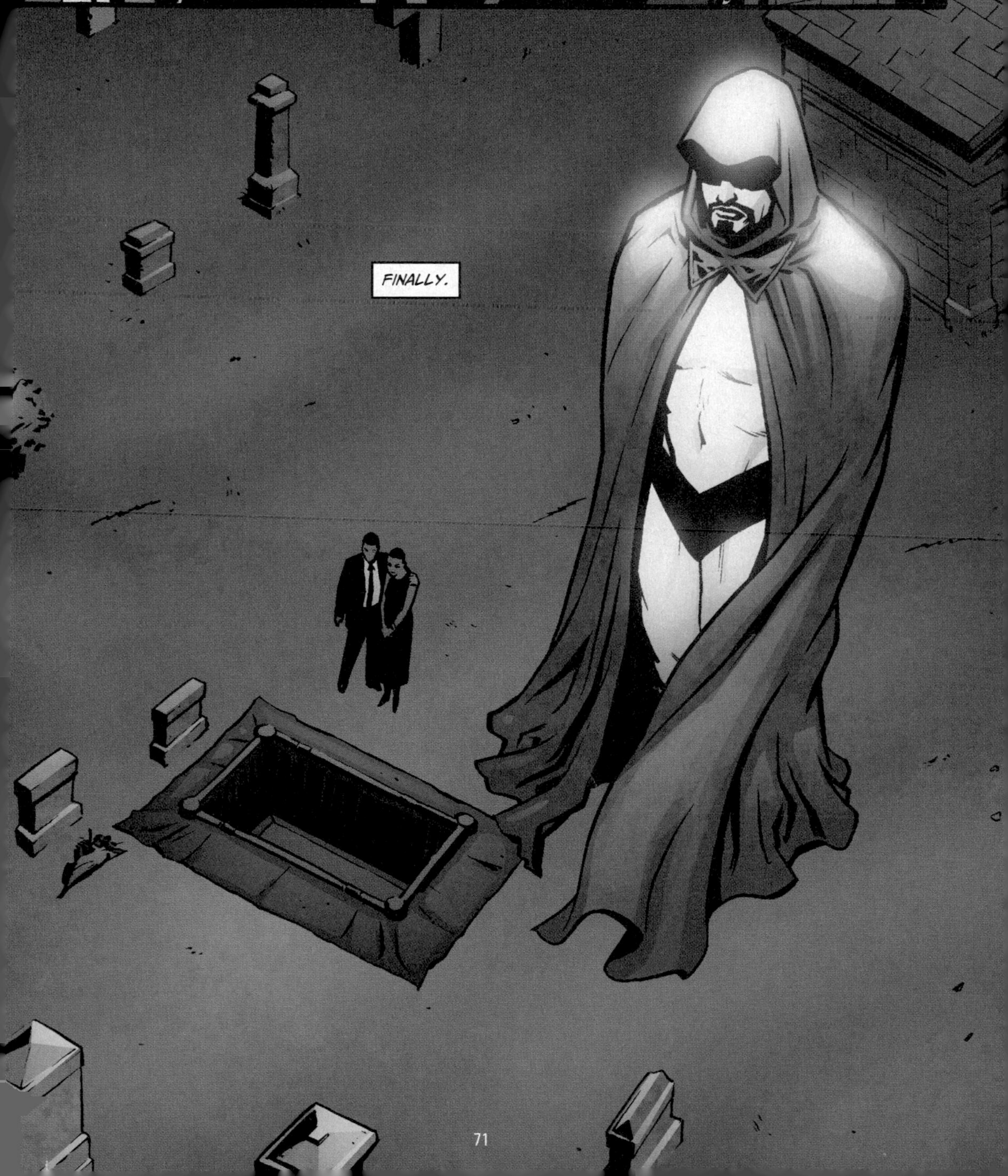
FINALLY.

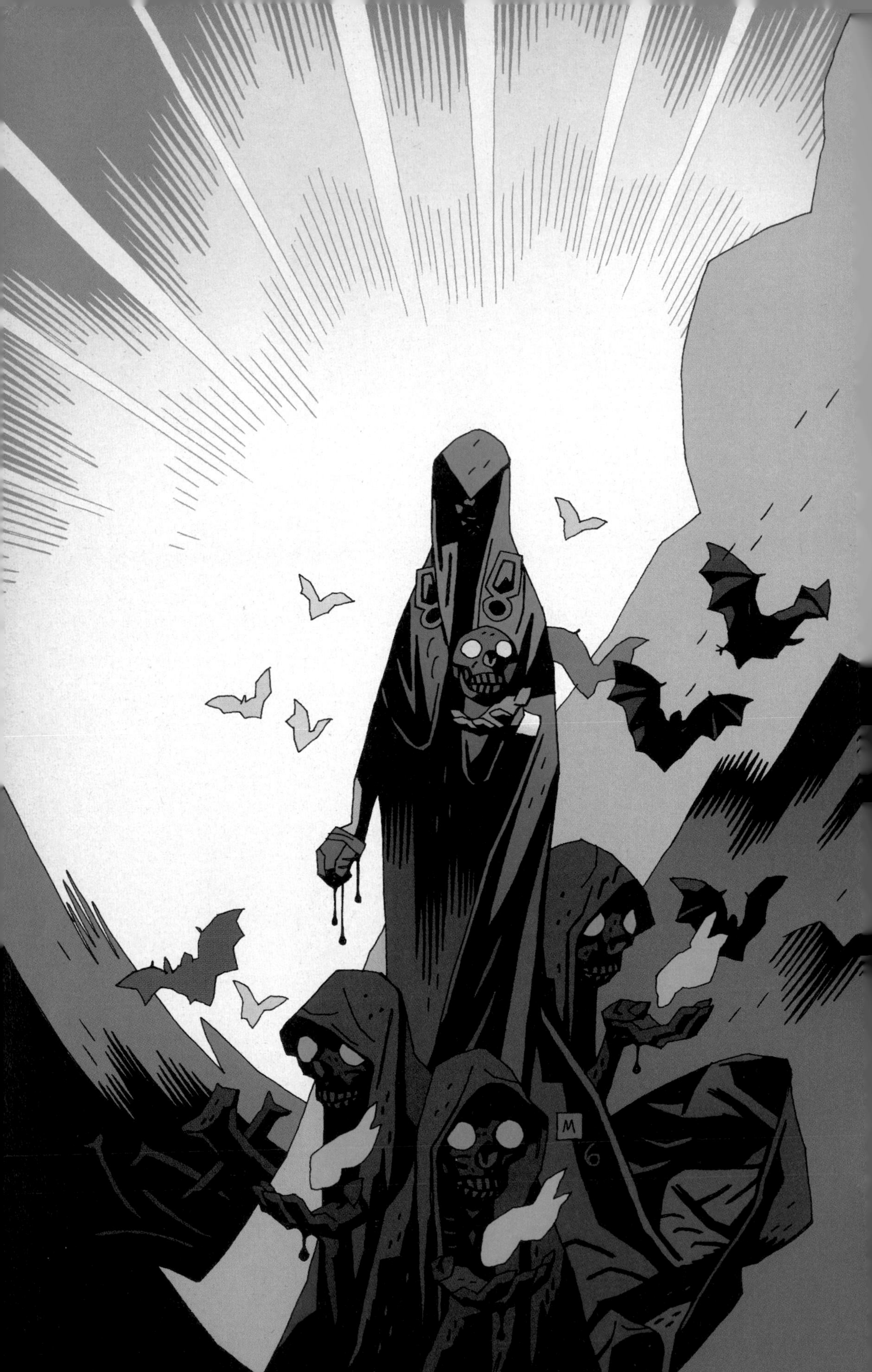

art by Mike Mignola & Dave Stewart

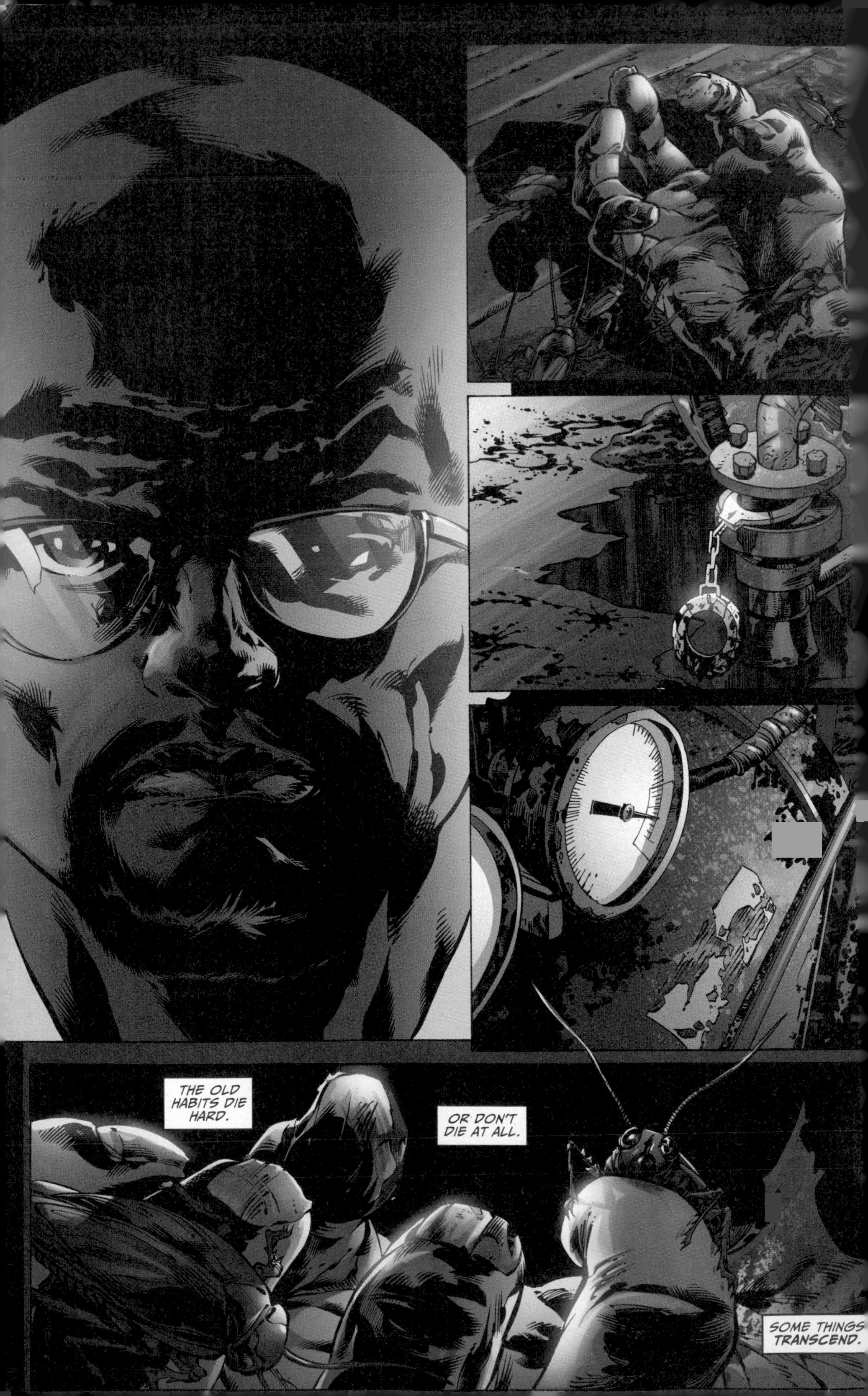
THE OLD HABITS DIE HARD.
OR DON'T DIE AT ALL.
SOME THINGS TRANSCEND.

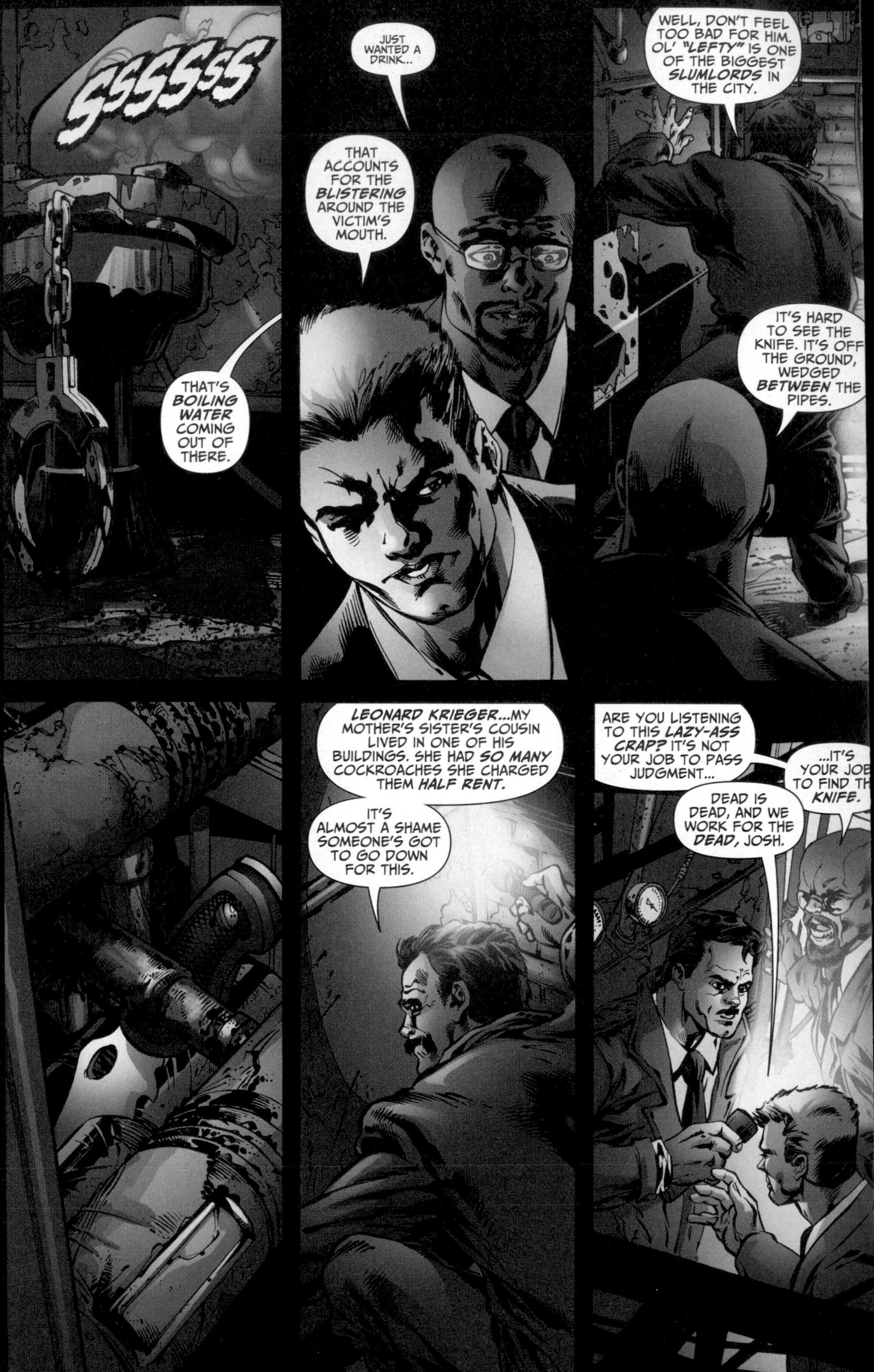
SSSSSS
THAT'S BOILING WATER COMING OUT OF THERE.
JUST WANTED A DRINK...
THAT ACCOUNTS FOR THE BLISTERING AROUND THE VICTIM'S MOUTH.
WELL, DON'T FEEL TOO BAD FOR HIM. OL' "LEFTY" IS ONE OF THE BIGGEST SLUMLORDS IN THE CITY.
IT'S HARD TO SEE THE KNIFE. IT'S OFF THE GROUND, WEDGED BETWEEN THE PIPES.
LEONARD KRIEGER...MY MOTHER'S SISTER'S COUSIN LIVED IN ONE OF HIS BUILDINGS. SHE HAD SO MANY COCKROACHES SHE CHARGED THEM HALF RENT.
IT'S ALMOST A SHAME SOMEONE'S GOT TO GO DOWN FOR THIS.
ARE YOU LISTENING TO THIS LAZY-ASS CRAP? IT'S NOT YOUR JOB TO PASS JUDGMENT...
...IT'S YOUR JOB TO FIND THE KNIFE.
DEAD IS DEAD, AND WE WORK FOR THE DEAD, JOSH.

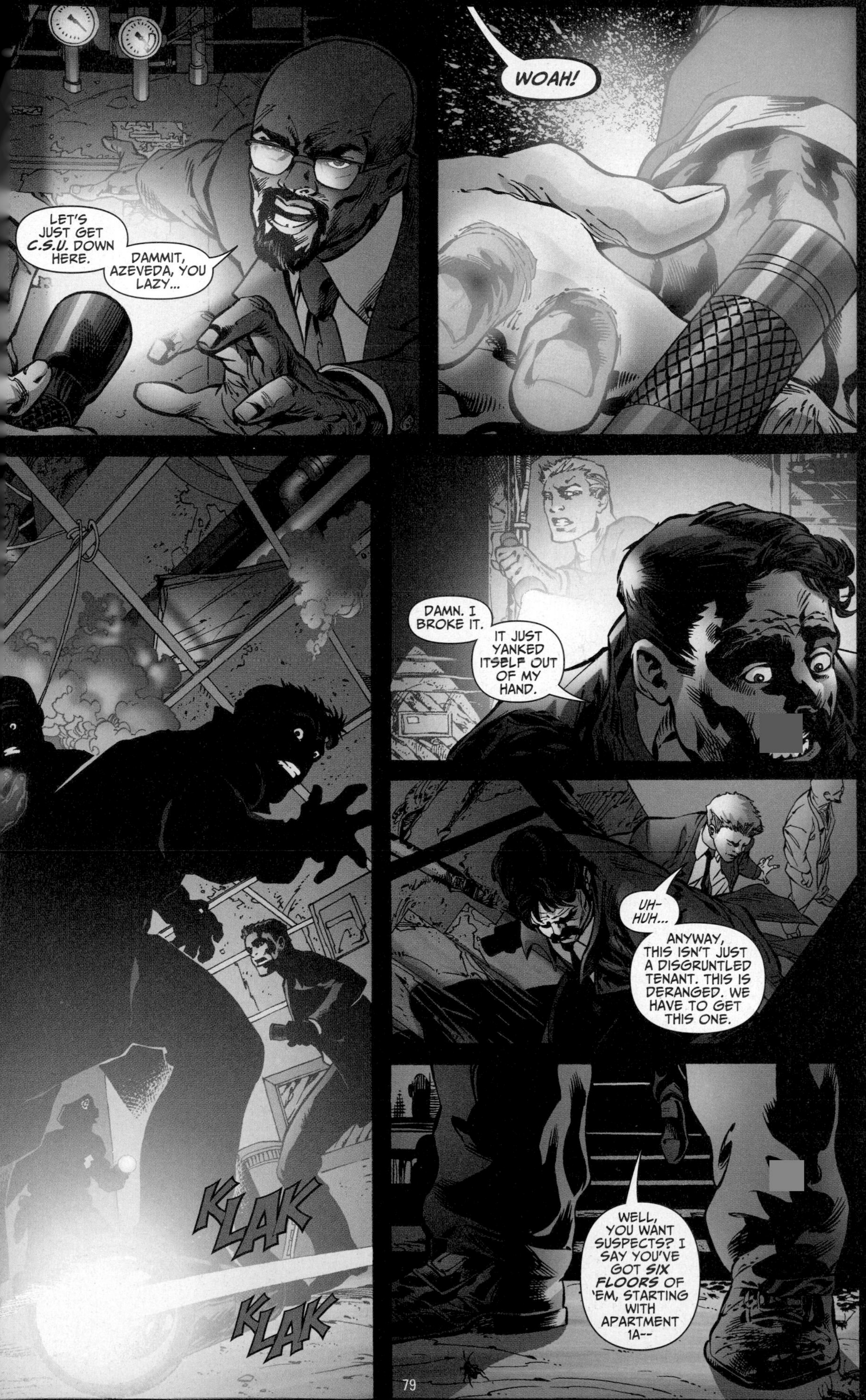
LET'S JUST GET C.S.U. DOWN HERE.
DAMMIT, AZEVEDA, YOU LAZY...
WOAH!
DAMN. I BROKE IT.
IT JUST YANKED ITSELF OUT OF MY HAND.
UH-HUH...
ANYWAY, THIS ISN'T JUST A DISGRUNTLED TENANT. THIS IS DERANGED. WE HAVE TO GET THIS ONE.
KLAK
KLAK
WELL, YOU WANT SUSPECTS? I SAY YOU'VE GOT SIX FLOORS OF 'EM, STARTING WITH APARTMENT 1A--

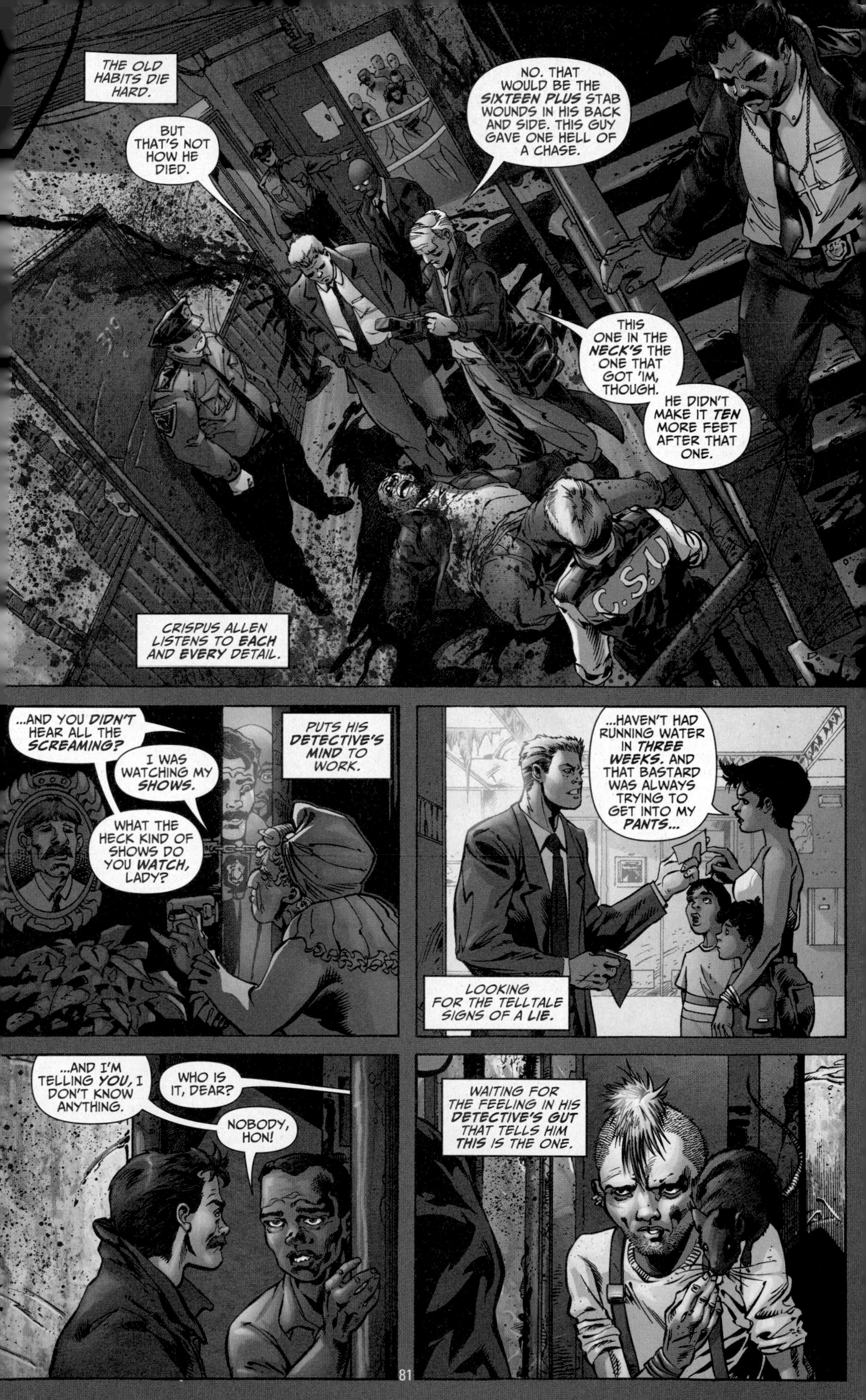

THE OLD HABITS DIE HARD.
BUT THAT'S NOT HOW HE DIED.
NO. THAT WOULD BE THE SIXTEEN PLUS STAB WOUNDS IN HIS BACK AND SIDE. THIS GUY GAVE ONE HELL OF A CHASE.
THIS ONE IN THE NECK'S THE ONE THAT GOT 'IM, THOUGH.
HE DIDN'T MAKE IT TEN MORE FEET AFTER THAT ONE.
C.S.U.
CRISPUS ALLEN LISTENS TO EACH AND EVERY DETAIL.
...AND YOU DIDN'T HEAR ALL THE SCREAMING?
I WAS WATCHING MY SHOWS.
WHAT THE HECK KIND OF SHOWS DO YOU WATCH, LADY?
PUTS HIS DETECTIVE'S MIND TO WORK.
...HAVEN'T HAD RUNNING WATER IN THREE WEEKS. AND THAT BASTARD WAS ALWAYS TRYING TO GET INTO MY PANTS...
LOOKING FOR THE TELLTALE SIGNS OF A LIE.
...AND I'M TELLING YOU, I DON'T KNOW ANYTHING.
WHO IS IT, DEAR?
NOBODY, HON!
WAITING FOR THE FEELING IN HIS DETECTIVE'S GUT THAT TELLS HIM THIS IS THE ONE.

ONLY HE NO LONGER HAS A DETECTIVE'S GUT.

INSTEAD, HE HAS A MONSTER.

...PIGS...

EVERY MOUTH IS SEALED TO THEM.

EVERY DOOR CLOSED.

SLAM!

THEY HAVE RULES. AND FOR EIGHTEEN YEARS HE FOLLOWED THEM, FOUGHT THEM, BENT THEM, BUT NEVER BROKE THEM.

THEY GAVE HIS LIFE MEANING. MADE HIS WORK RIGHTEOUS.

NOW THERE ARE NO BARRIERS TO STAND BETWEEN HIM AND THE TRUTH.

BUT THE TRUTH HAS BECOME HIS ENEMY.

WHEN HE LEARNS THE TRUTH, THE MONSTER WILL COME OUT.

AND HAVE ITS BUCKET OF BLOOD.

ANOTHER OLD HABIT...

...A HELPING HAND...

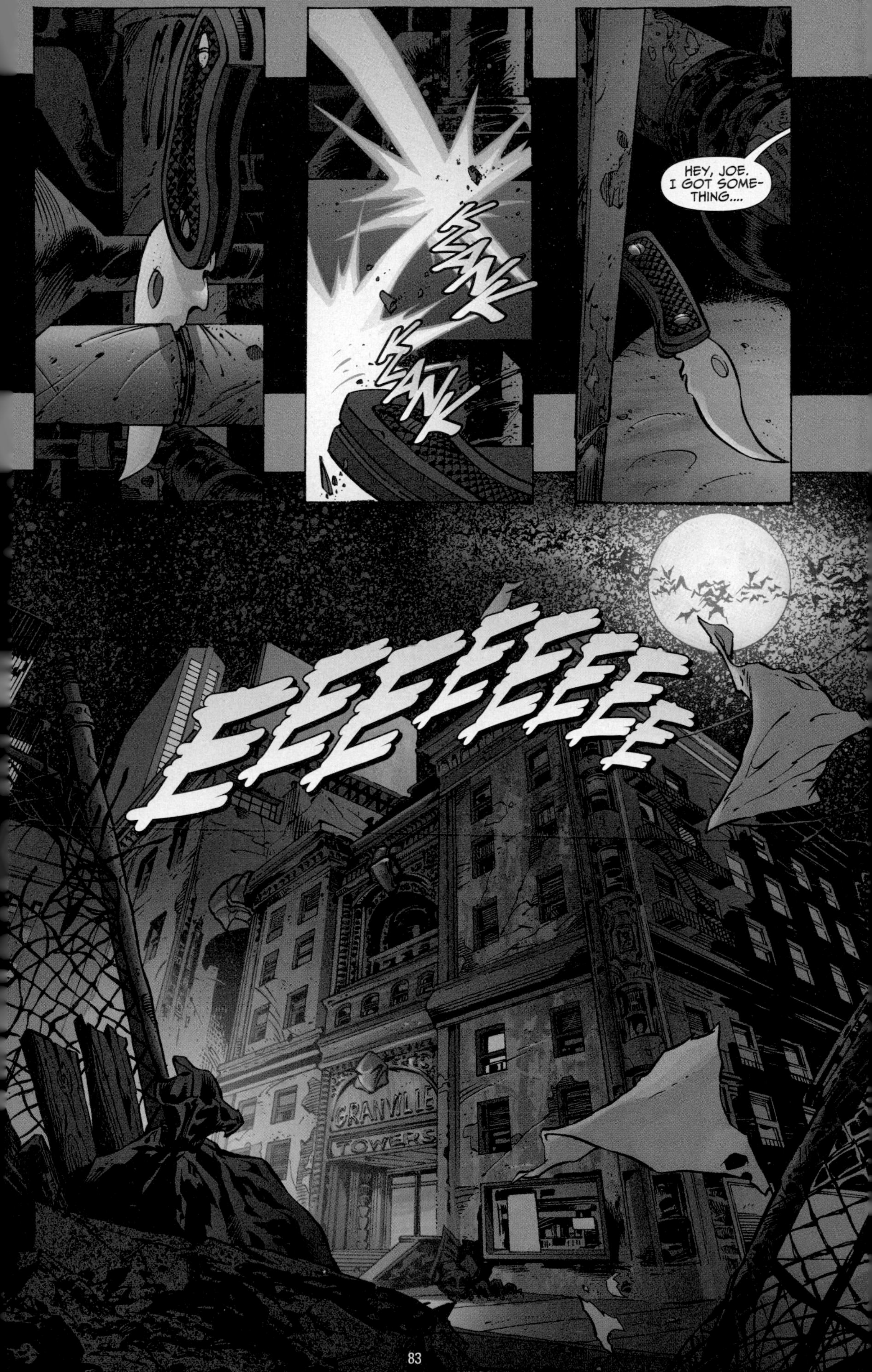
KLANK
KLANK
HEY, JOE. I GOT SOME-THING....
EEEEEEEEE
GRANVILLE TOWERS

EEEEEEEE

EEEEEEEE

SHHHHH. IT'S OKAY. SHHHH.

IT'S JUST A *DREAM.* JUST A BAD DREAM.

CASEY! CASEY! ARE YOU OKAY?

IT WAS THE *MAN.* HE WAS RUNNING... RUNNING WITH THE KNIFE.

IT WAS JUST A *DREAM,* SWEETIE.

HE WAS GOING TO KILL ME.

RON... IT'S *TOO* MUCH FOR HER.

IT'S NOT FAIR.

WHAT'S TOO MUCH, CHERYL? WHAT?!

DON'T YELL AT ME. I'M JUST SAYING--

WHAT?! WHAT ARE YOU SAYING?!

IT'S A LITTLE LATE TO BE SAYING ANYTHING, DON'T YOU THINK?

DID THEY DO THIS?

HIS STOMACH TWISTS IN KNOTS. THE MONSTER WILL NOT BE KIND.

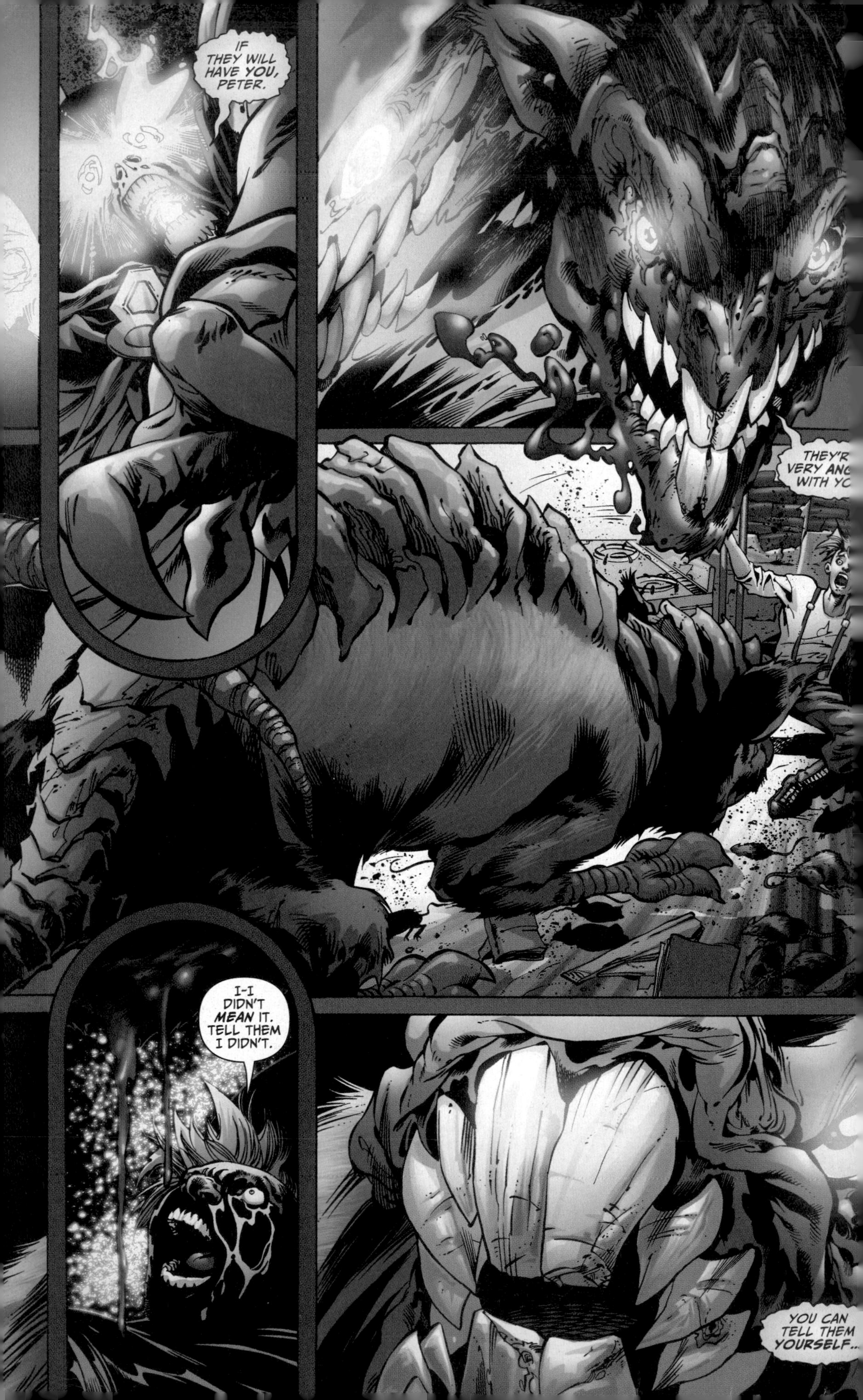
IF THEY WILL HAVE YOU, PETER.
THEY'R VERY ANG WITH YO
I-I DIDN'T MEAN IT. TELL THEM I DIDN'T.
YOU CAN TELL THEM YOURSELF...

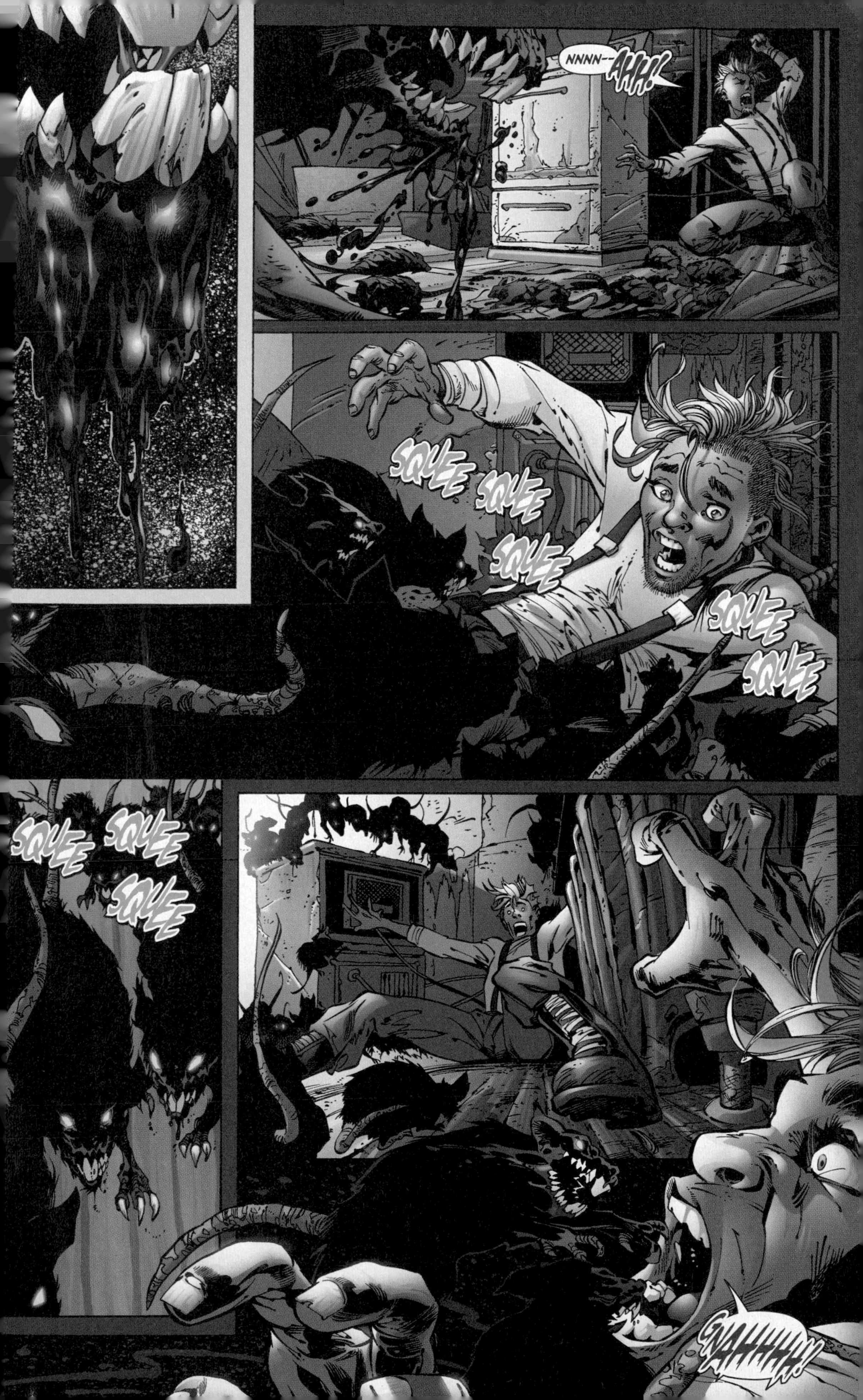

NNNN--AHH!
SQUEE SQUEE
SQUEE
SQUEE
SQUEE
SQUEE SQUEE
SQUEE
GNAHHHH!

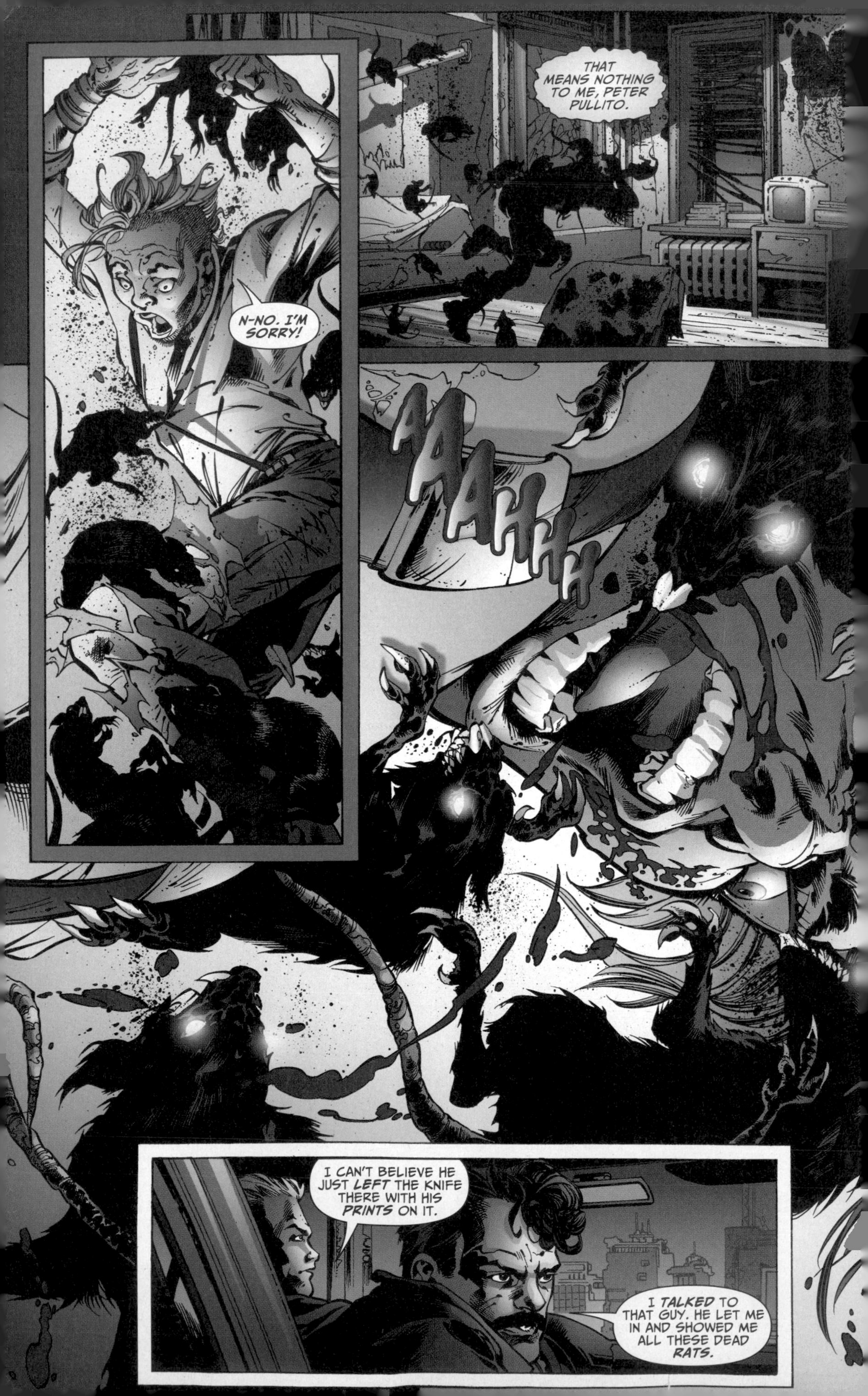
THAT MEANS NOTHING TO ME, PETER PULLITO.
N-NO. I'M SORRY!
AAAHHHH
I CAN'T BELIEVE HE JUST LEFT THE KNIFE THERE WITH HIS PRINTS ON IT.
I TALKED TO THAT GUY. HE LET ME IN AND SHOWED ME ALL THESE DEAD RATS.

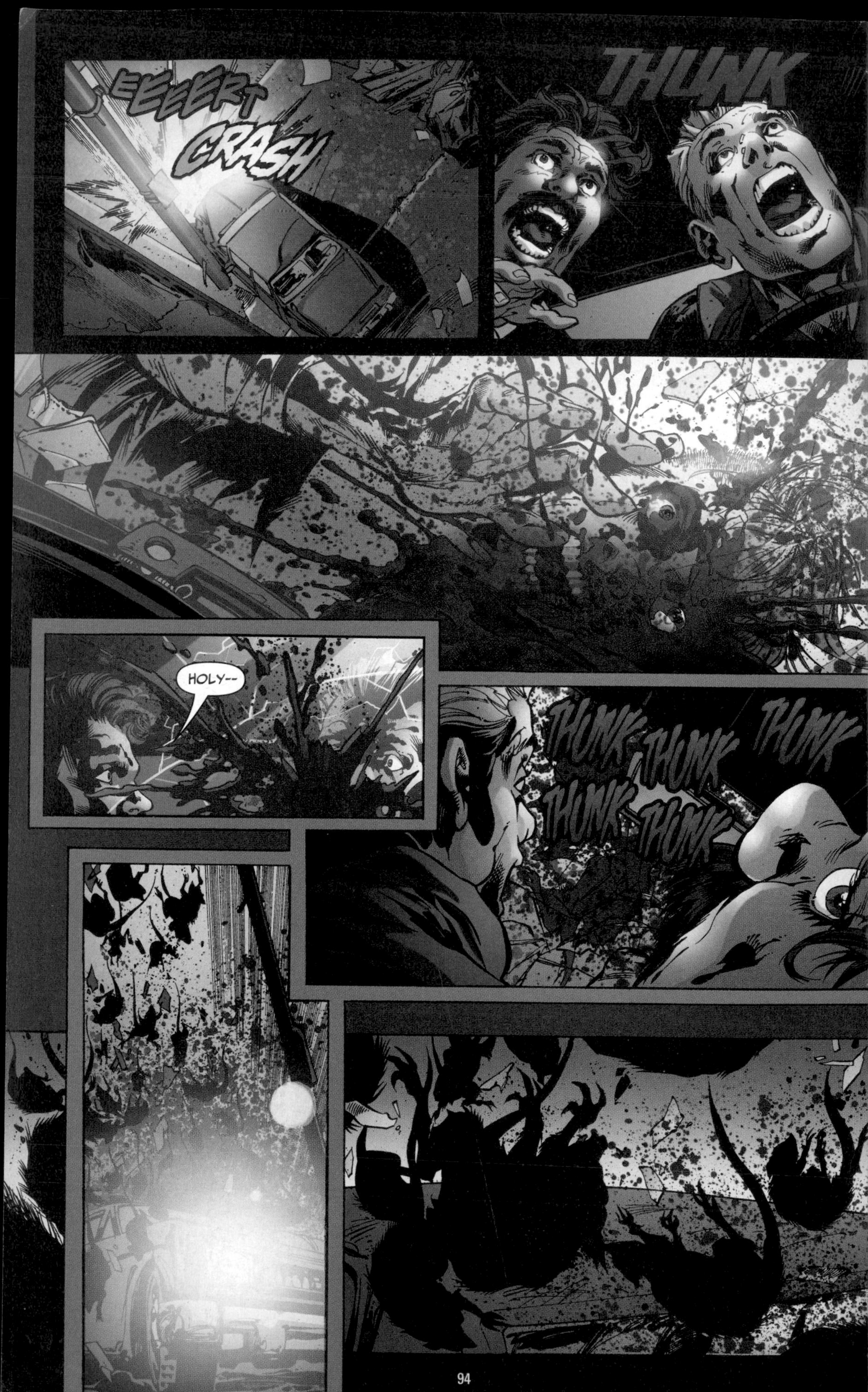
EEEEERT
CRASH
THUNK
HOLY--
THUNK
THUNK
THUNK
THUNK
THUNK

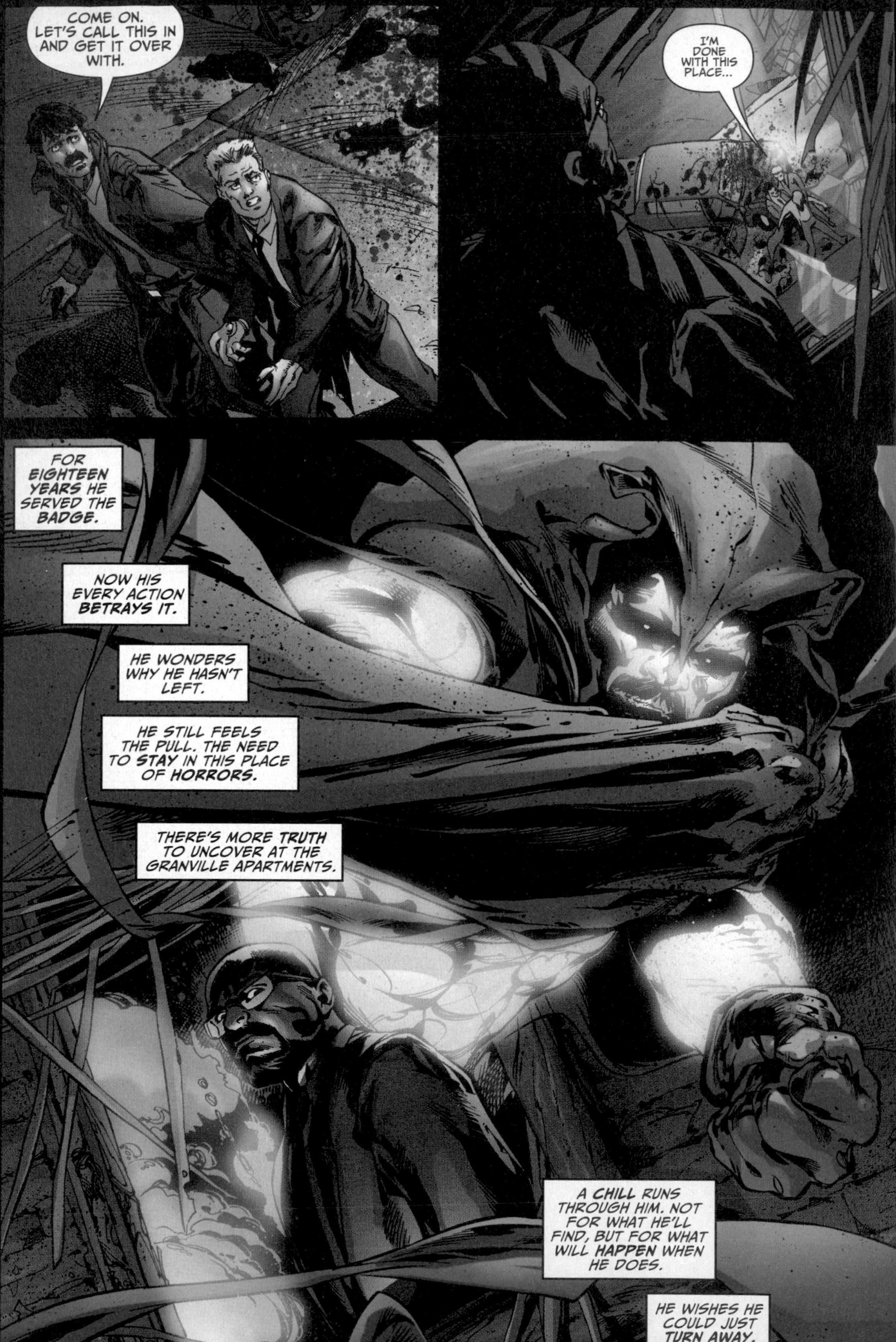
COME ON. LET'S CALL THIS IN AND GET IT OVER WITH.
I'M DONE WITH THIS PLACE...
FOR EIGHTEEN YEARS HE SERVED THE BADGE.
NOW HIS EVERY ACTION BETRAYS IT.
HE WONDERS WHY HE HASN'T LEFT.
HE STILL FEELS THE PULL. THE NEED TO STAY IN THIS PLACE OF HORRORS.
THERE'S MORE TRUTH TO UNCOVER AT THE GRANVILLE APARTMENTS.
A CHILL RUNS THROUGH HIM. NOT FOR WHAT HE'LL FIND, BUT FOR WHAT WILL HAPPEN WHEN HE DOES.
HE WISHES HE COULD JUST TURN AWAY.
BUT THE OLD HABITS DIE HARD.

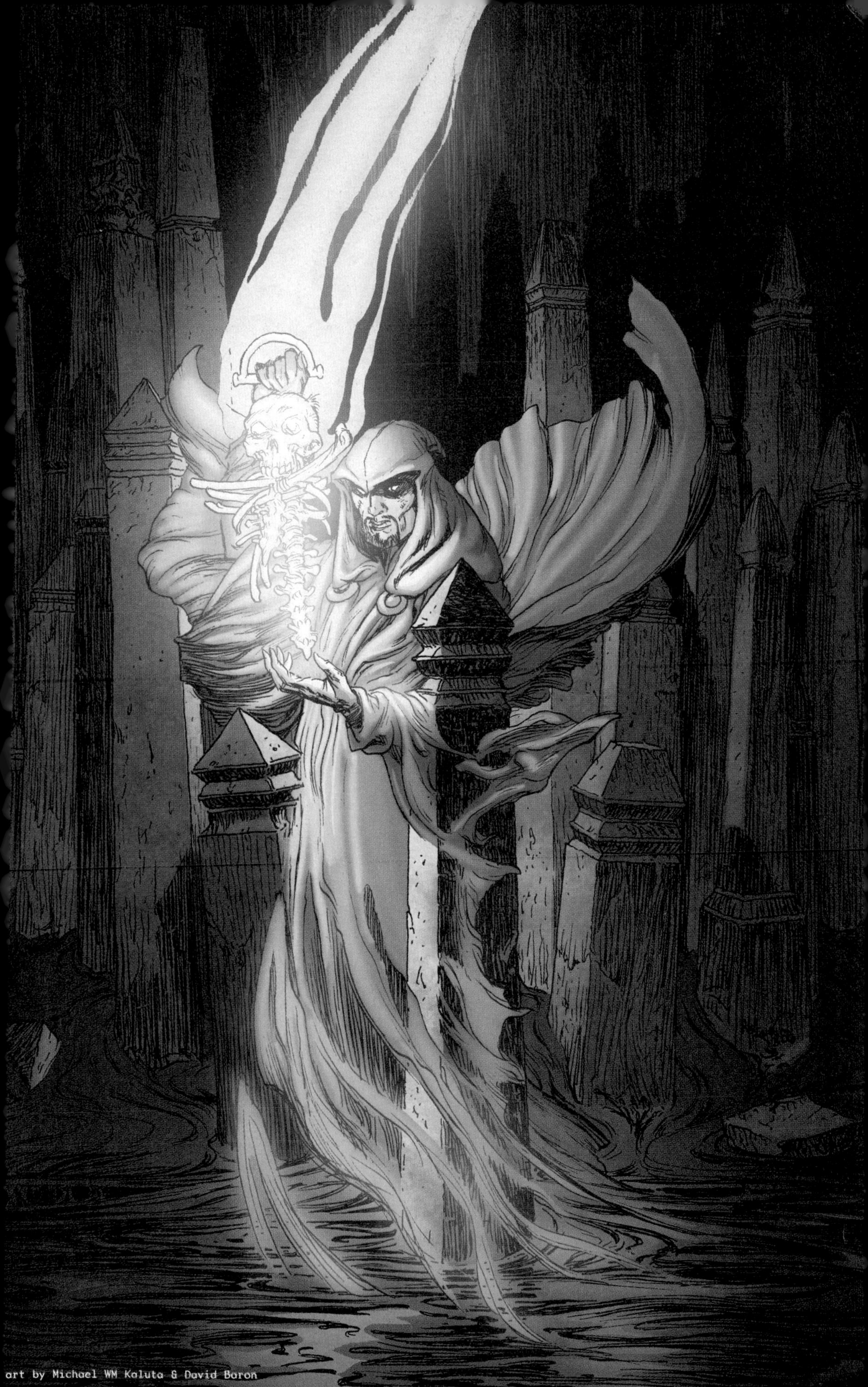

art by Michael WM Kaluta & David Baron

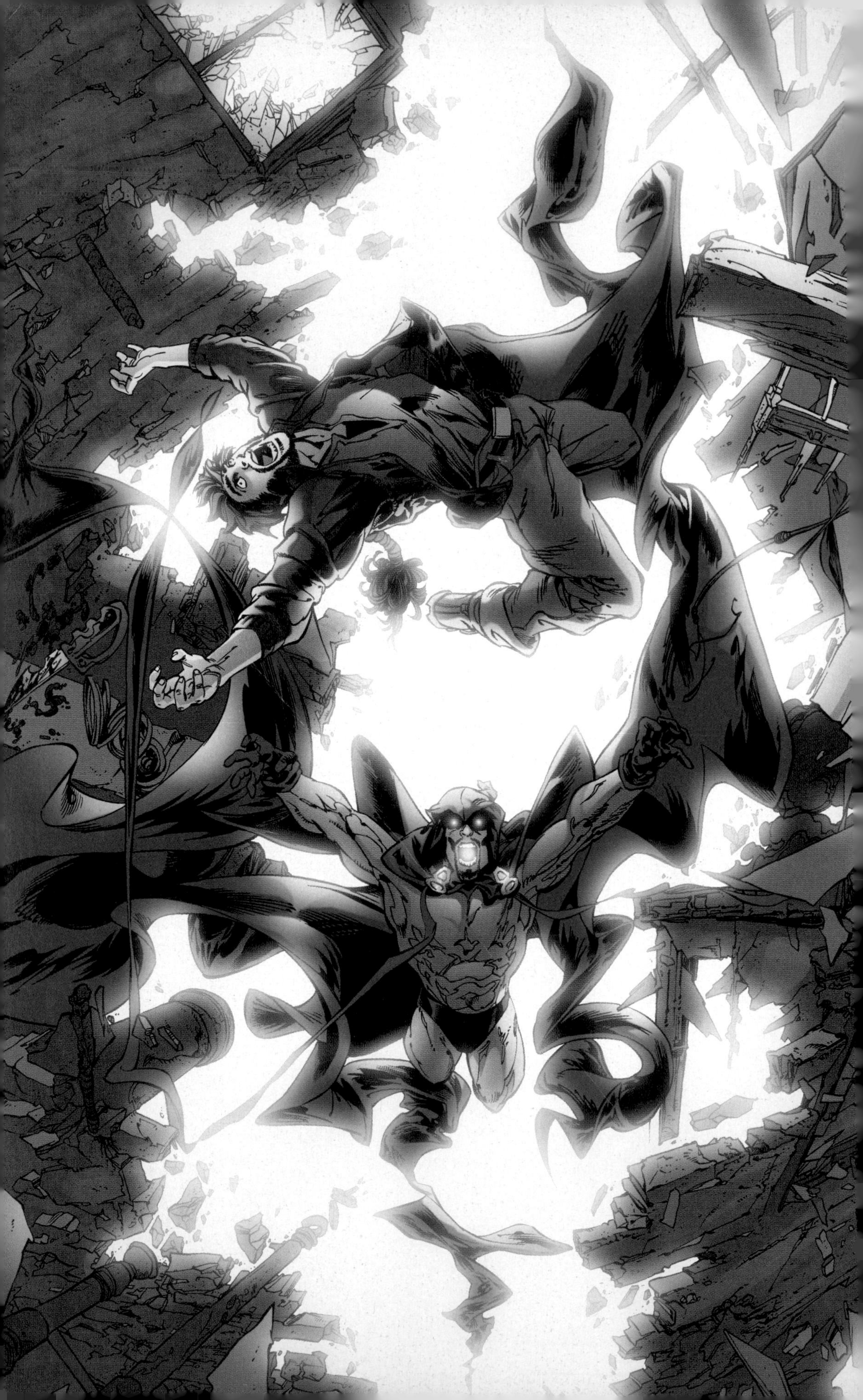

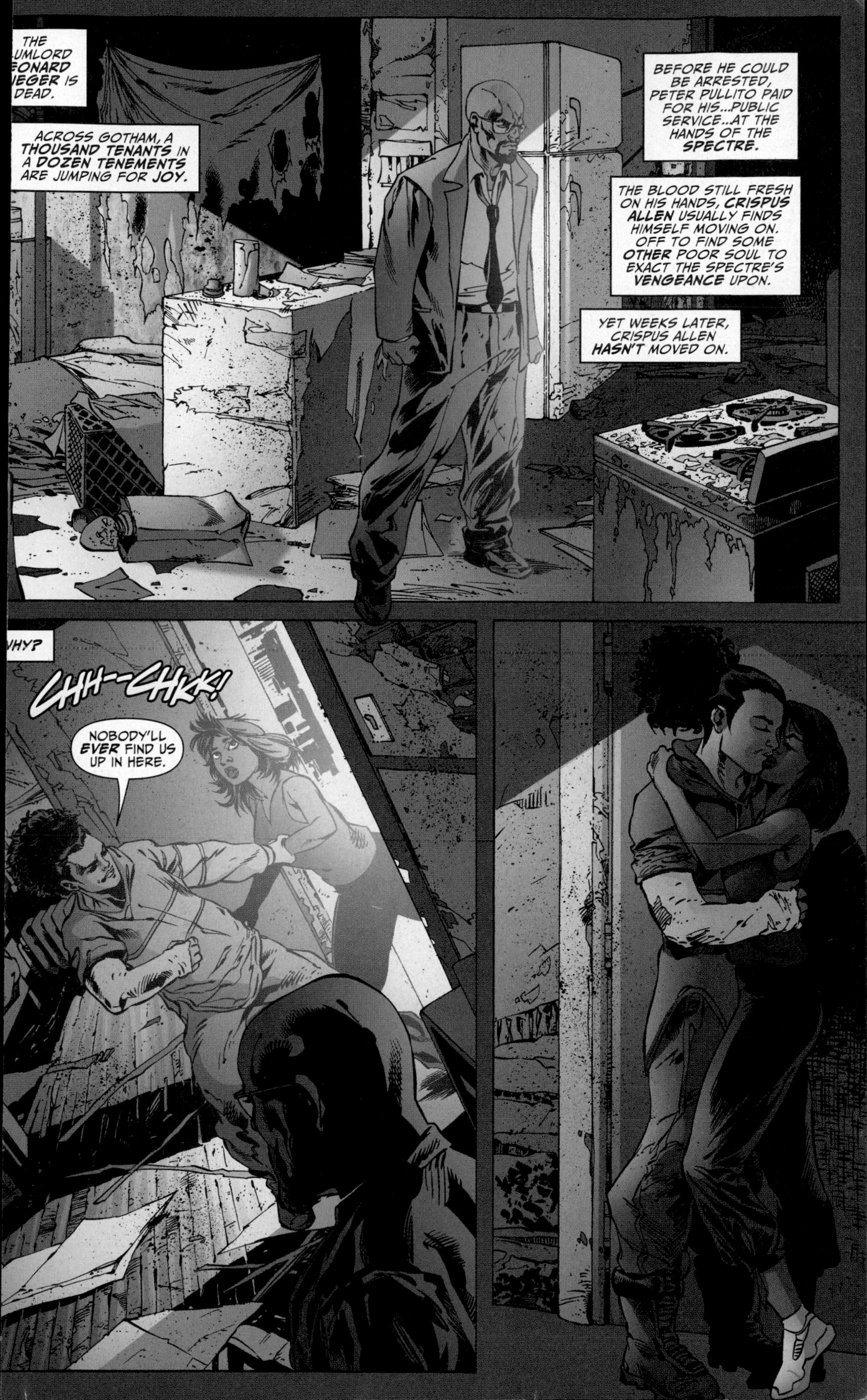
THE
UMLORD
EONARD
IEGER IS
DEAD.
ACROSS GOTHAM, A THOUSAND TENANTS IN A DOZEN TENEMENTS ARE JUMPING FOR JOY.
BEFORE HE COULD BE ARRESTED, PETER PULLITO PAID FOR HIS...PUBLIC SERVICE...AT THE HANDS OF THE SPECTRE.
THE BLOOD STILL FRESH ON HIS HANDS, CRISPUS ALLEN USUALLY FINDS HIMSELF MOVING ON. OFF TO FIND SOME OTHER POOR SOUL TO EXACT THE SPECTRE'S VENGEANCE UPON.
YET WEEKS LATER, CRISPUS ALLEN HASN'T MOVED ON.
HY?
CHH--CHKK!
NOBODY'LL EVER FIND US UP IN HERE.

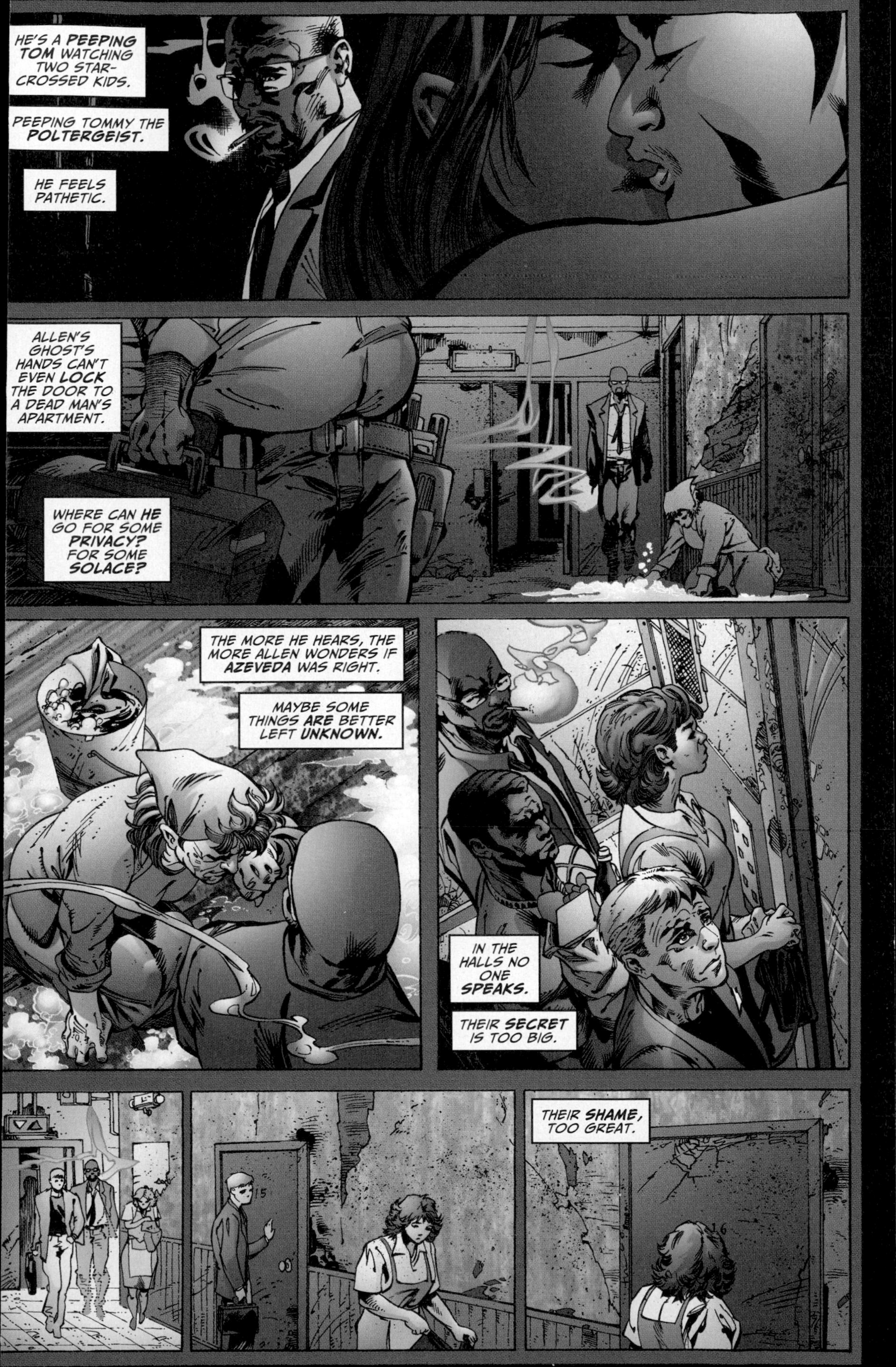

HE'S A PEEPING TOM WATCHING TWO STAR-CROSSED KIDS.
PEEPING TOMMY THE POLTERGEIST.
HE FEELS PATHETIC.
ALLEN'S GHOST'S HANDS CAN'T EVEN LOCK THE DOOR TO A DEAD MAN'S APARTMENT.
WHERE CAN HE GO FOR SOME PRIVACY? FOR SOME SOLACE?
THE MORE HE HEARS, THE MORE ALLEN WONDERS IF AZEVEDA WAS RIGHT.
MAYBE SOME THINGS ARE BETTER LEFT UNKNOWN.
IN THE HALLS NO ONE SPEAKS.
THEIR SECRET IS TOO BIG.
15
THEIR SHAME, TOO GREAT.
16

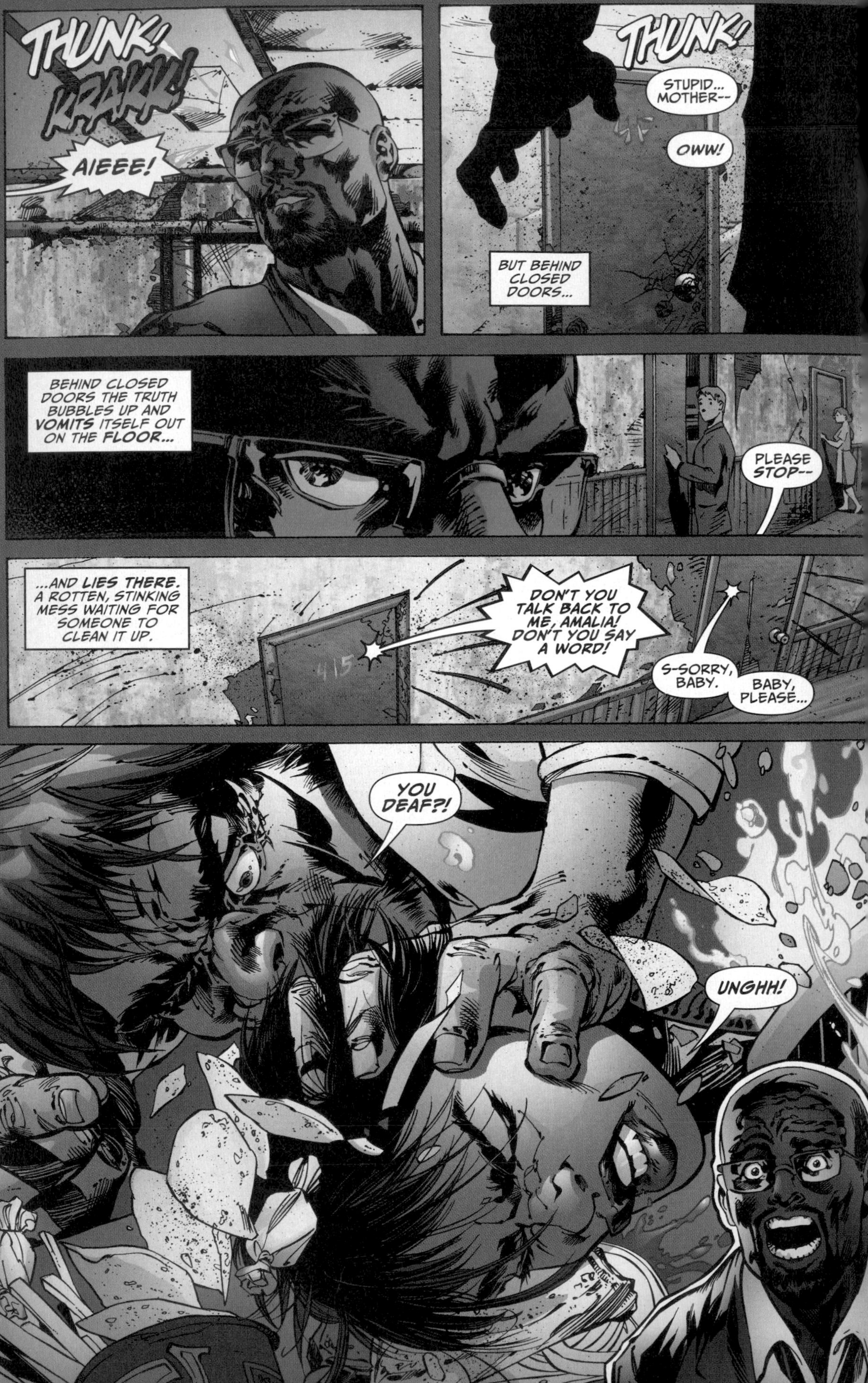
THUNK!
KRAKK!
AIEEE!
THUNK!
STUPID... MOTHER--
OWW!
BUT BEHIND CLOSED DOORS...
BEHIND CLOSED DOORS THE TRUTH BUBBLES UP AND VOMITS ITSELF OUT ON THE FLOOR...
PLEASE STOP--
...AND LIES THERE. A ROTTEN, STINKING MESS WAITING FOR SOMEONE TO CLEAN IT UP.
DON'T YOU TALK BACK TO ME, AMALIA! DON'T YOU SAY A WORD!
415
S-SORRY, BABY.
BABY, PLEASE...
YOU DEAF?!
UNGHH!

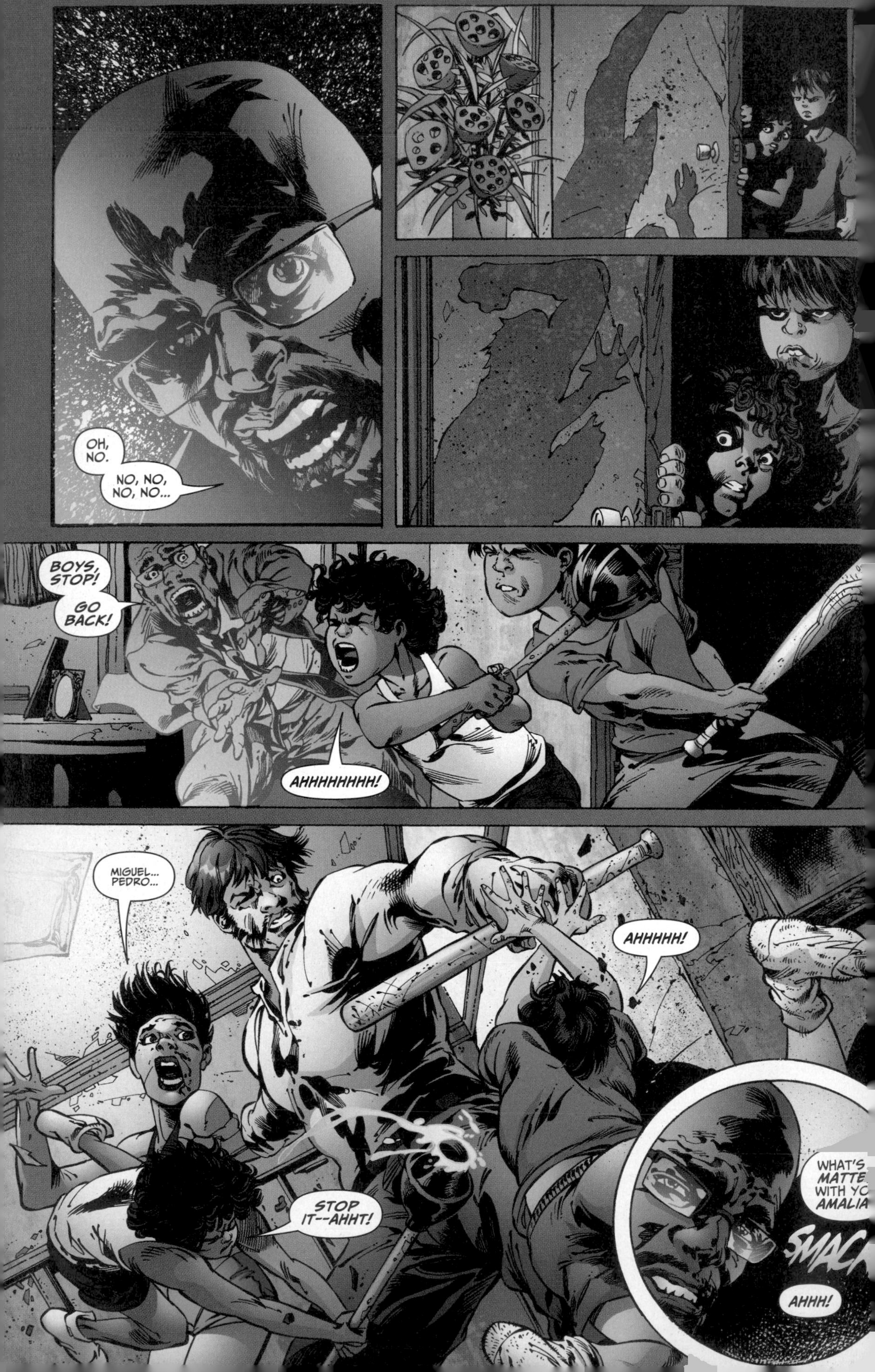
OH, NO.
NO, NO, NO, NO...
BOYS, STOP!
GO BACK!
AHHHHHHHH!
MIGUEL... PEDRO...
AHHHHH!
STOP IT--AHHT!
WHAT'S MATTE WITH YO AMALIA
SMACK
AHHH!

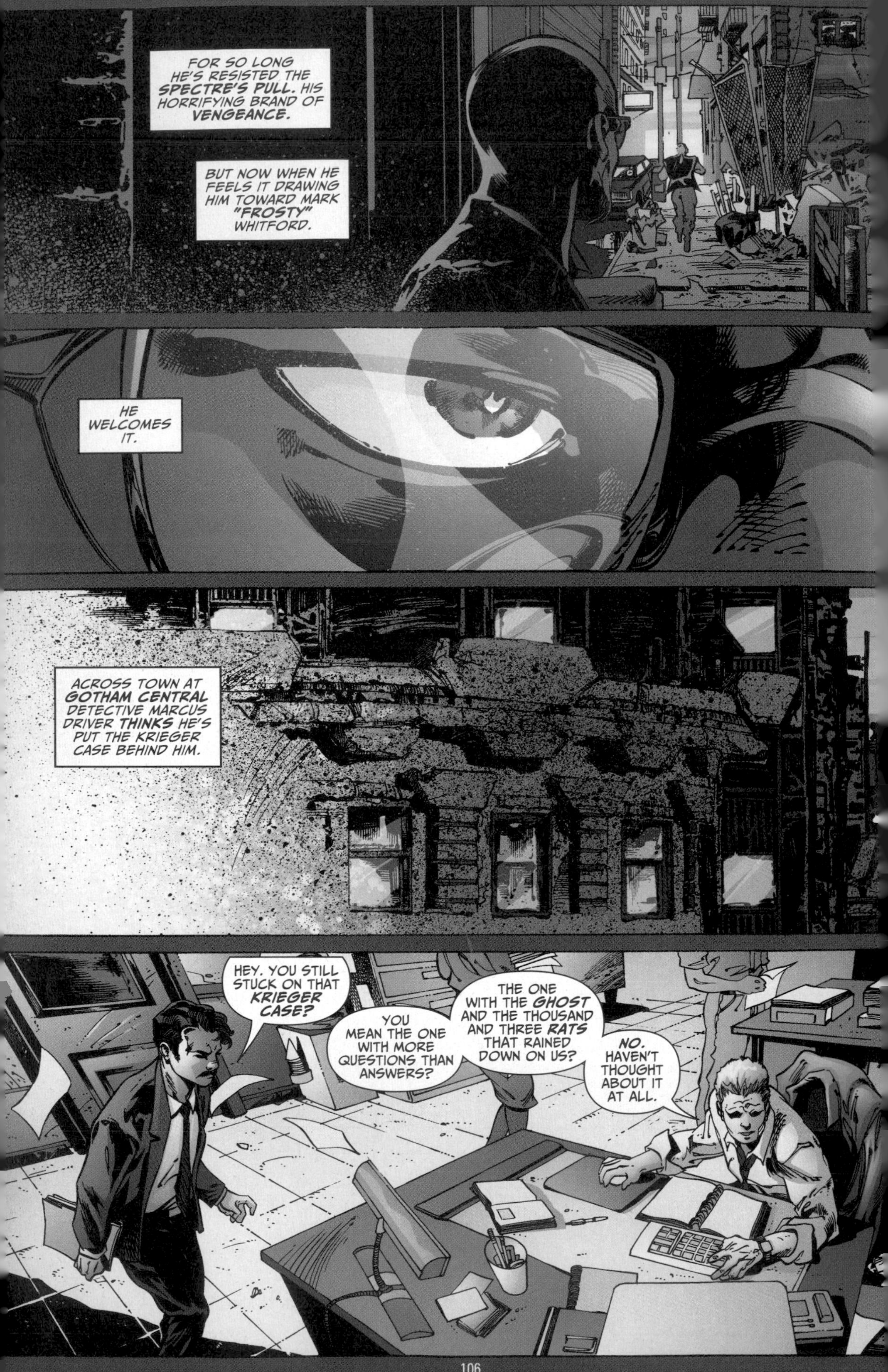
FOR SO LONG HE'S RESISTED THE SPECTRE'S PULL. HIS HORRIFYING BRAND OF VENGEANCE.
BUT NOW WHEN HE FEELS IT DRAWING HIM TOWARD MARK "FROSTY" WHITFORD.
HE WELCOMES IT.
ACROSS TOWN AT GOTHAM CENTRAL DETECTIVE MARCUS DRIVER THINKS HE'S PUT THE KRIEGER CASE BEHIND HIM.
HEY. YOU STILL STUCK ON THAT KRIEGER CASE?
YOU MEAN THE ONE WITH MORE QUESTIONS THAN ANSWERS?
THE ONE WITH THE GHOST AND THE THOUSAND AND THREE RATS THAT RAINED DOWN ON US?
NO. HAVEN'T THOUGHT ABOUT IT AT ALL.

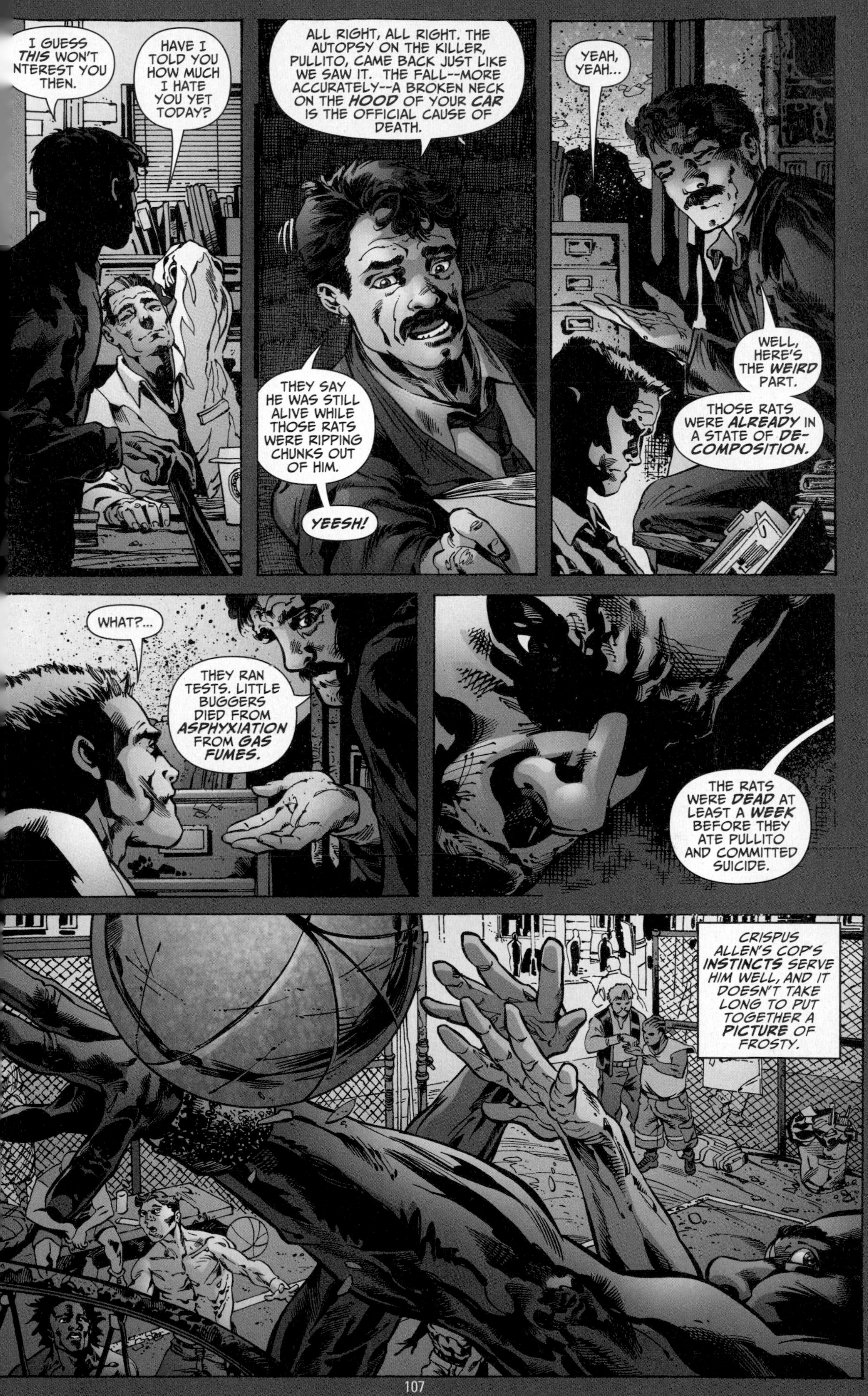
I GUESS THIS WON'T INTEREST YOU THEN.
HAVE I TOLD YOU HOW MUCH I HATE YOU YET TODAY?
ALL RIGHT, ALL RIGHT. THE AUTOPSY ON THE KILLER, PULLITO, CAME BACK JUST LIKE WE SAW IT. THE FALL--MORE ACCURATELY--A BROKEN NECK ON THE HOOD OF YOUR CAR IS THE OFFICIAL CAUSE OF DEATH.
THEY SAY HE WAS STILL ALIVE WHILE THOSE RATS WERE RIPPING CHUNKS OUT OF HIM.
YEESH!
YEAH, YEAH...
WELL, HERE'S THE WEIRD PART.
THOSE RATS WERE ALREADY IN A STATE OF DE-COMPOSITION.
WHAT?...
THEY RAN TESTS. LITTLE BUGGERS DIED FROM ASPHYXIATION FROM GAS FUMES.
THE RATS WERE DEAD AT LEAST A WEEK BEFORE THEY ATE PULLITO AND COMMITTED SUICIDE.
CRISPUS ALLEN'S COP'S INSTINCTS SERVE HIM WELL, AND IT DOESN'T TAKE LONG TO PUT TOGETHER A PICTURE OF FROSTY.

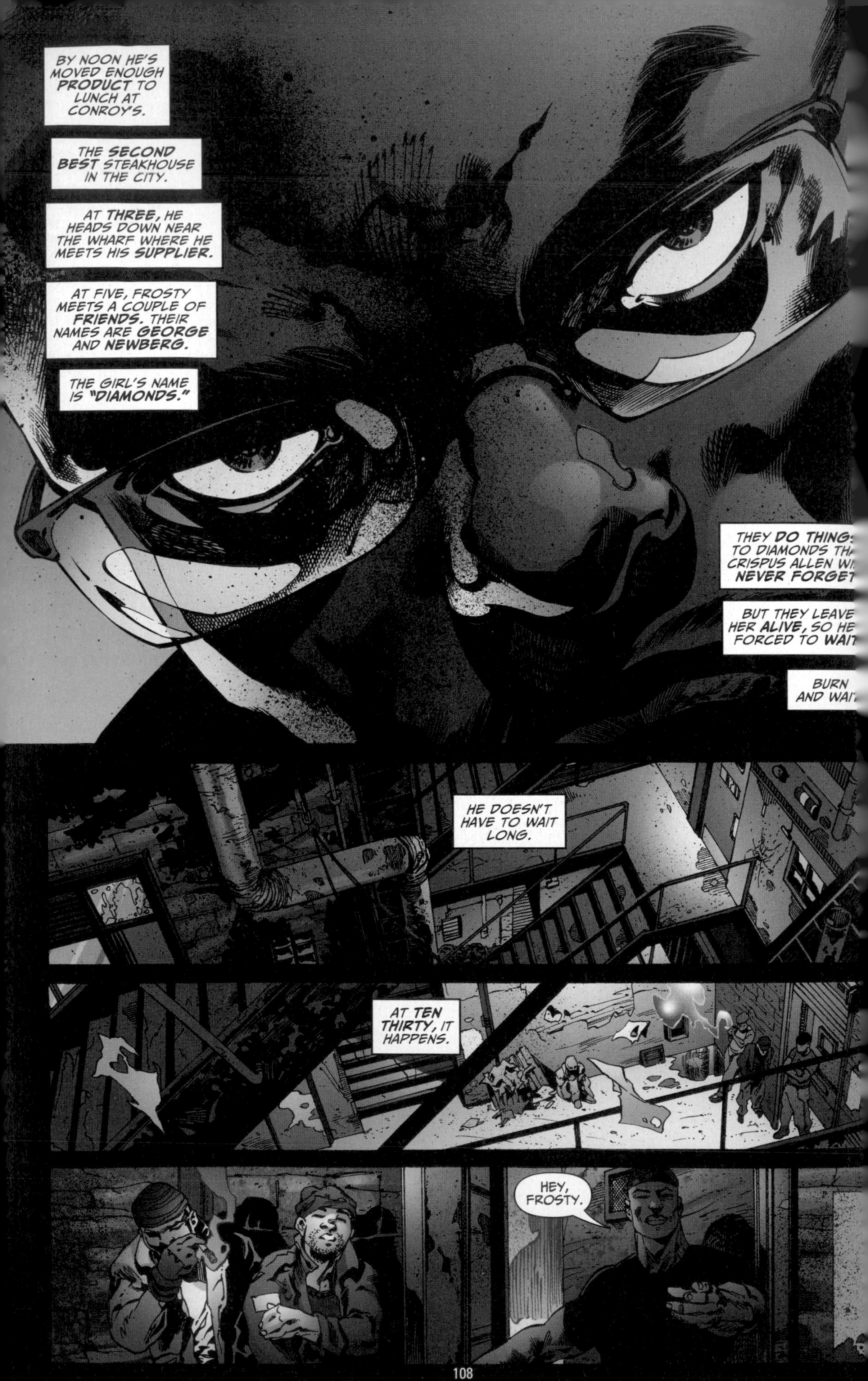
BY NOON HE'S MOVED ENOUGH PRODUCT TO LUNCH AT CONROY'S.
THE SECOND BEST STEAKHOUSE IN THE CITY.
AT THREE, HE HEADS DOWN NEAR THE WHARF WHERE HE MEETS HIS SUPPLIER.
AT FIVE, FROSTY MEETS A COUPLE OF FRIENDS. THEIR NAMES ARE GEORGE AND NEWBERG.
THE GIRL'S NAME IS "DIAMONDS."
THEY DO THING TO DIAMONDS TH CRISPUS ALLEN W NEVER FORGE
BUT THEY LEAVE HER ALIVE, SO HE FORCED TO WAI
BURN AND WAI
HE DOESN'T HAVE TO WAIT LONG.
AT TEN THIRTY, IT HAPPENS.
HEY, FROSTY.

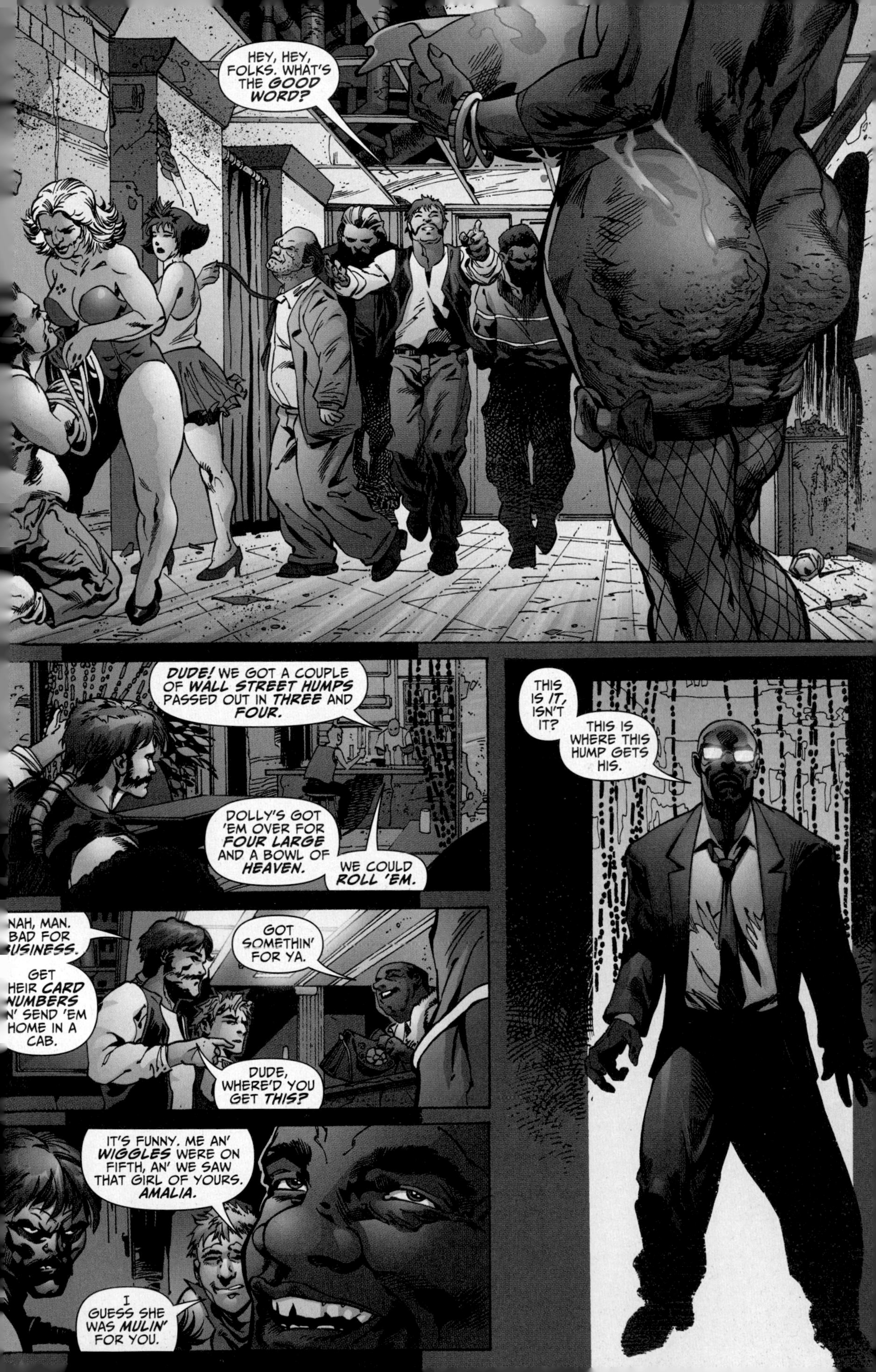
HEY, HEY, FOLKS. WHAT'S THE GOOD WORD?
DUDE! WE GOT A COUPLE OF WALL STREET HUMPS PASSED OUT IN THREE AND FOUR.
DOLLY'S GOT 'EM OVER FOR FOUR LARGE AND A BOWL OF HEAVEN.
WE COULD ROLL 'EM.
NAH, MAN. BAD FOR BUSINESS.
GET THEIR CARD NUMBERS AN' SEND 'EM HOME IN A CAB.
GOT SOMETHIN' FOR YA.
DUDE, WHERE'D YOU GET THIS?
IT'S FUNNY. ME AN' WIGGLES WERE ON FIFTH, AN' WE SAW THAT GIRL OF YOURS. AMALIA.
I GUESS SHE WAS MULIN' FOR YOU.
THIS IS IT, ISN'T IT?
THIS IS WHERE THIS HUMP GETS HIS.

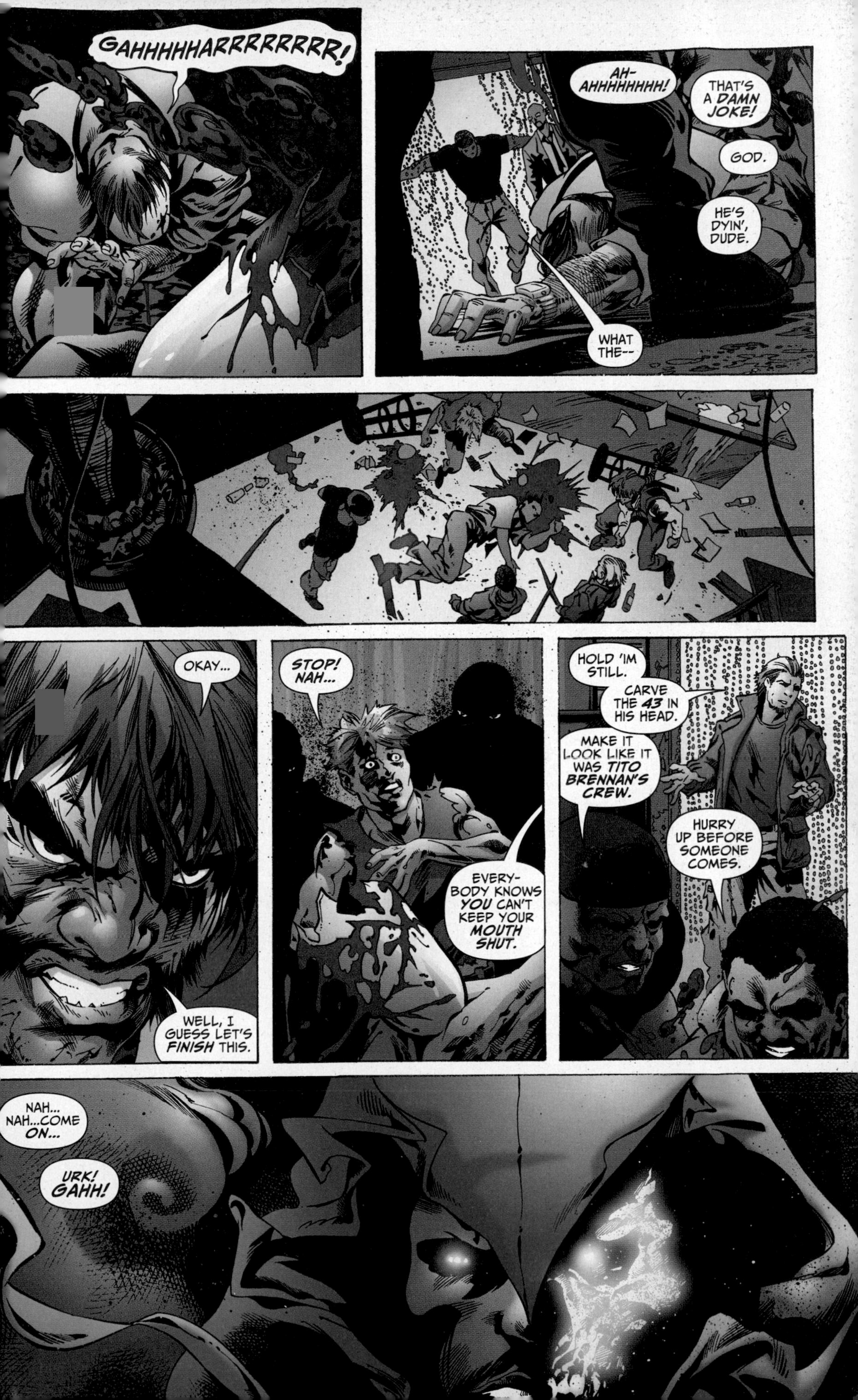
GAHHHHHARRRRRRR!
AH-AHHHHHHHH!
THAT'S A DAMN JOKE!
GOD.
HE'S DYIN', DUDE.
WHAT THE--
OKAY...
WELL, I GUESS LET'S FINISH THIS.
STOP! NAH...
EVERY-BODY KNOWS YOU CAN'T KEEP YOUR MOUTH SHUT.
HOLD 'IM STILL.
CARVE THE 43 IN HIS HEAD.
MAKE IT LOOK LIKE IT WAS TITO BRENNAN'S CREW.
HURRY UP BEFORE SOMEONE COMES.
NAH... NAH...COME ON...
URK! GAHH!

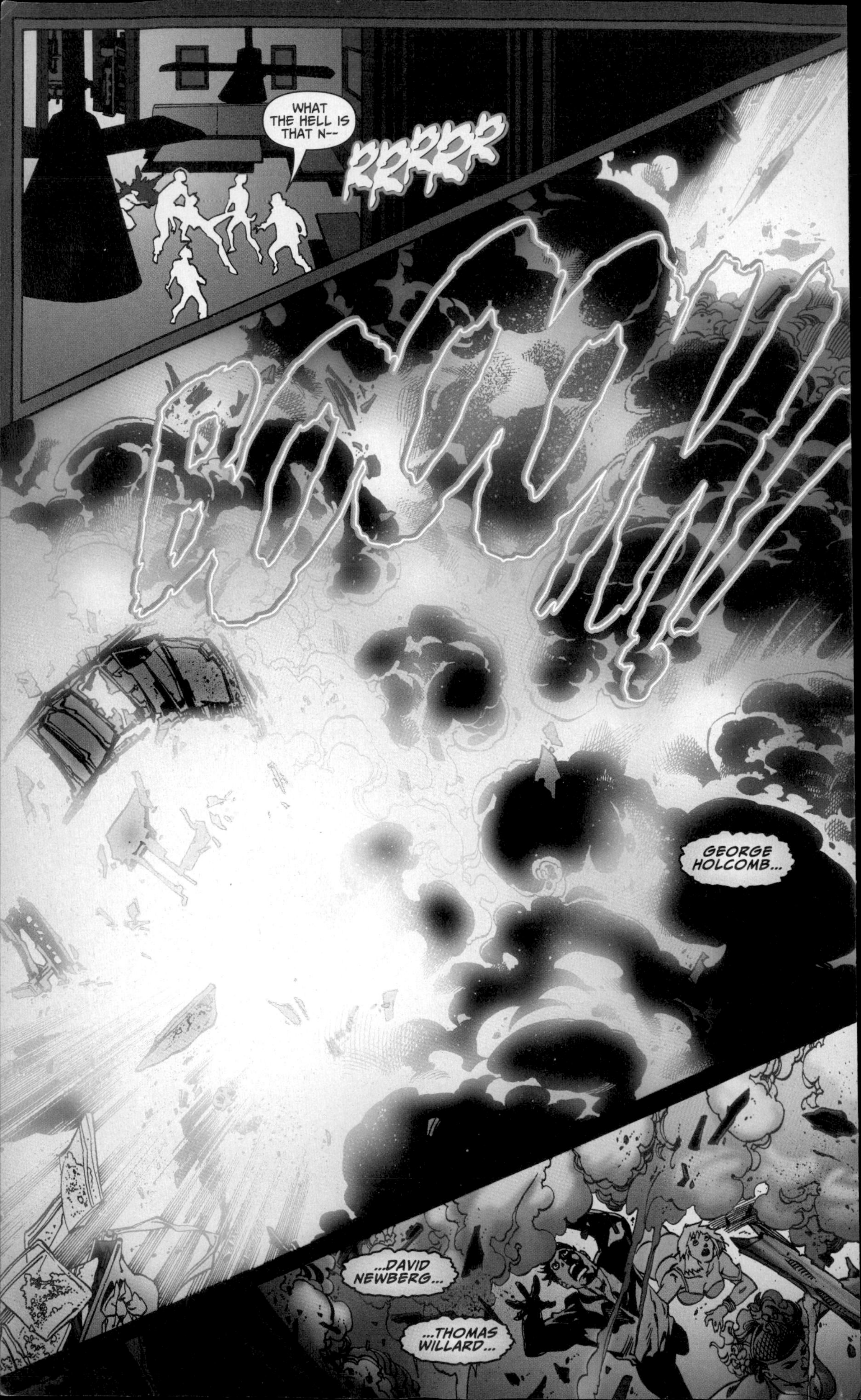
WHAT THE HELL IS THAT N--
RRRRR
BOOOM
GEORGE HOLCOMB...
...DAVID NEWBERG...
...THOMAS WILLARD...

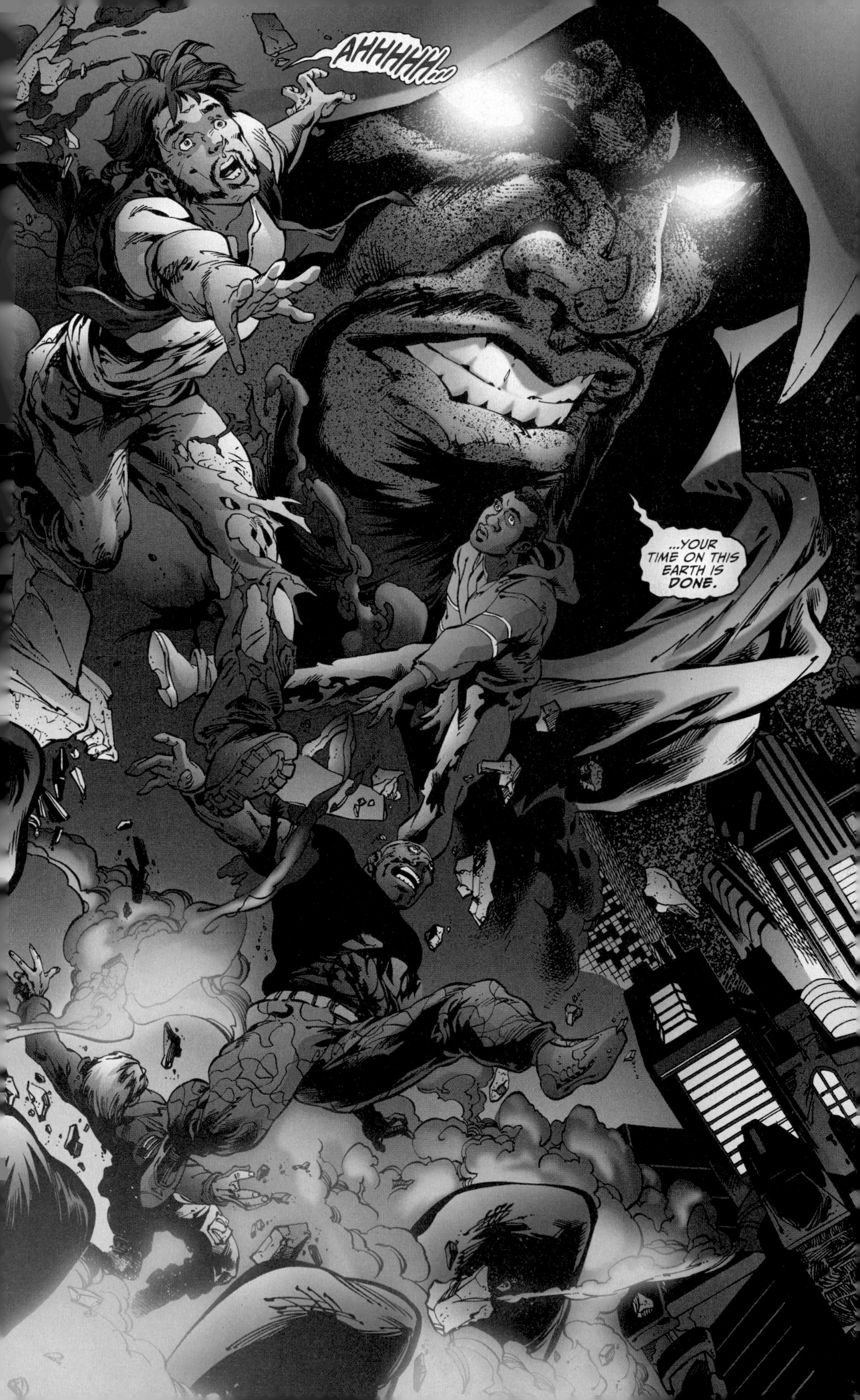
AHHHH...
...YOUR TIME ON THIS EARTH IS DONE.

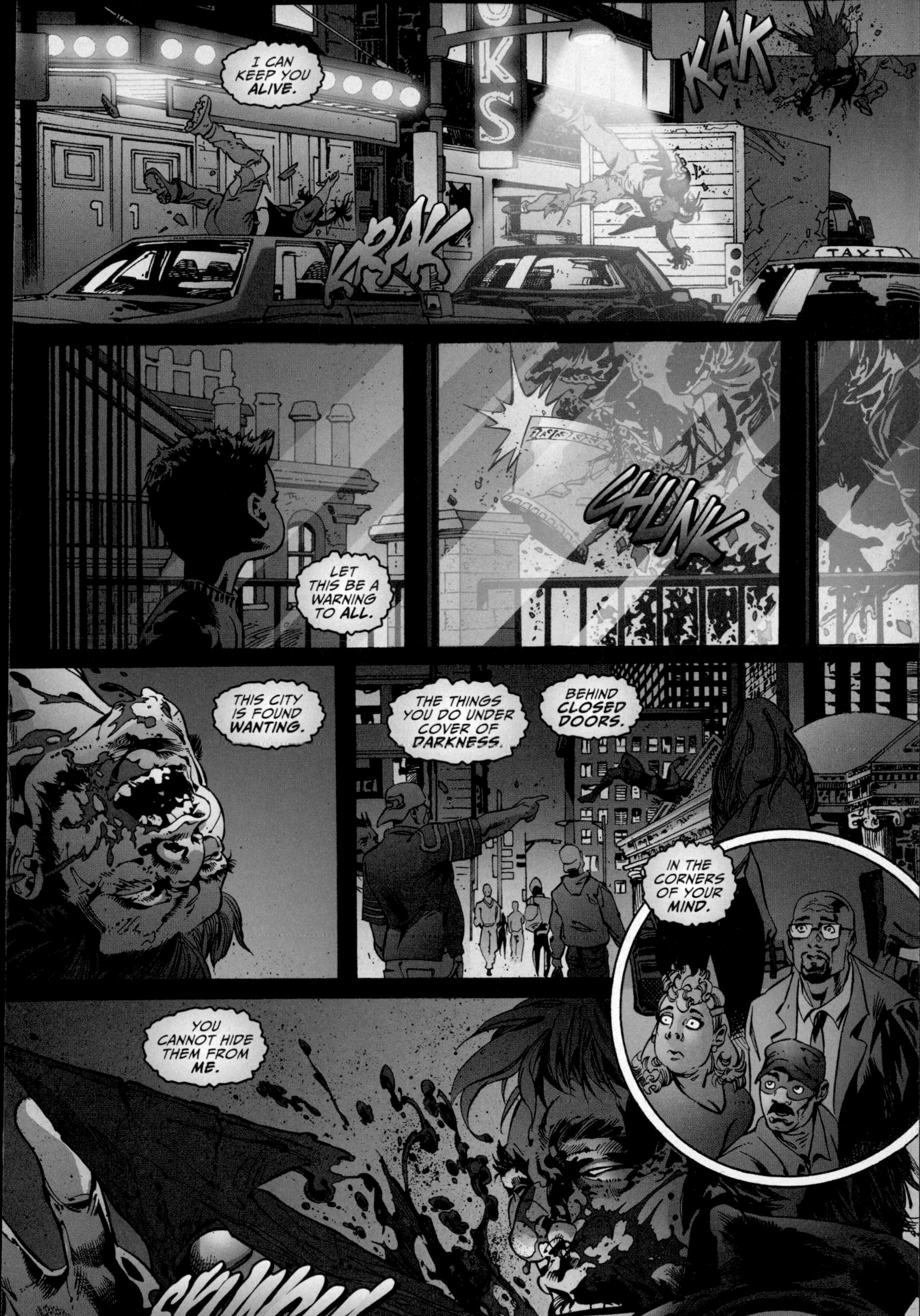

I CAN KEEP YOU ALIVE.
KAK
KRAK
LET THIS BE A WARNING TO ALL.
CHUNK
THIS CITY IS FOUND WANTING.
THE THINGS YOU DO UNDER COVER OF DARKNESS.
BEHIND CLOSED DOORS.
IN THE CORNERS OF YOUR MIND.
YOU CANNOT HIDE THEM FROM ME.
SKUNCH!

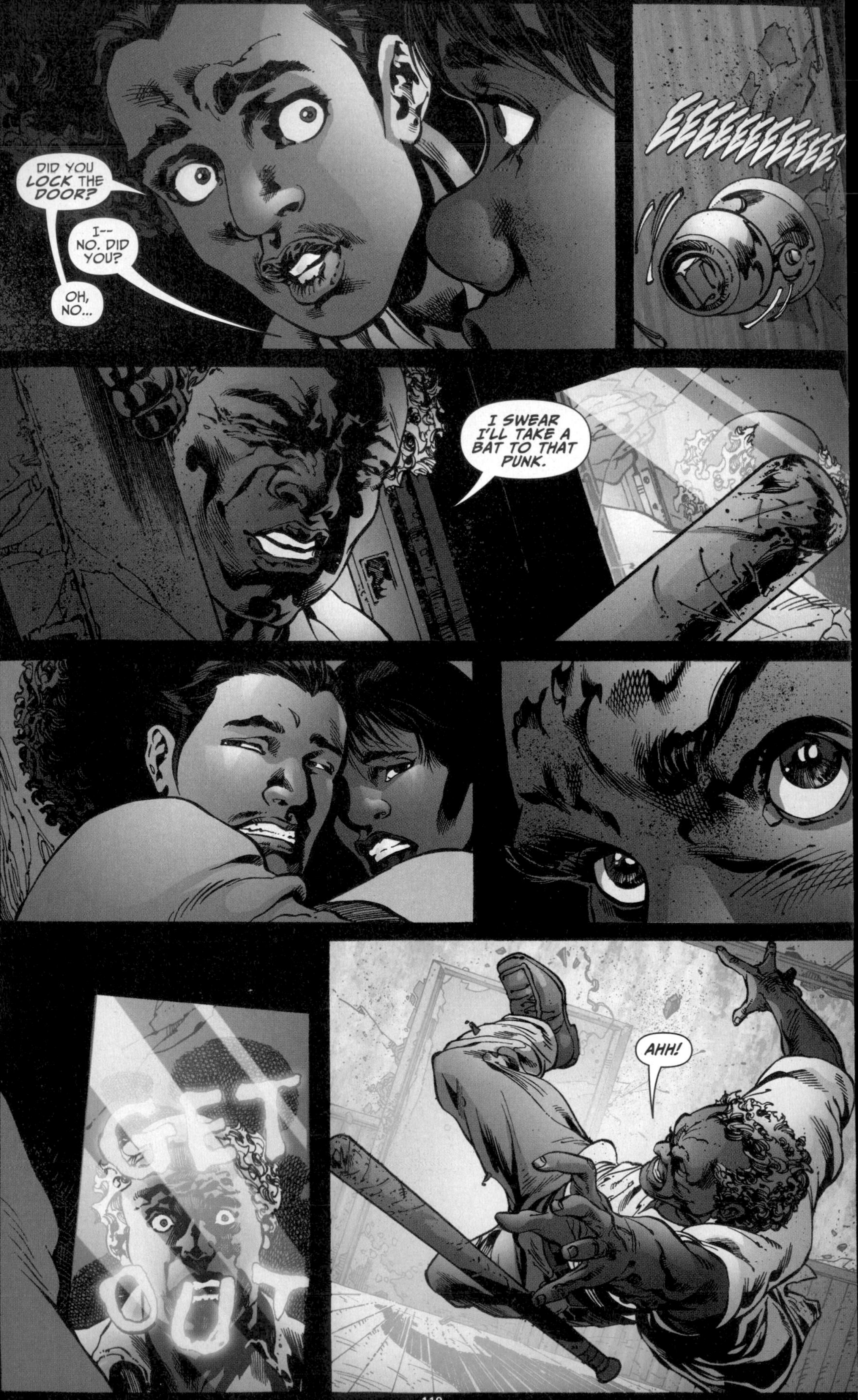

DID YOU LOCK THE DOOR?
I-- NO. DID YOU?
OH, NO...
EEEEEEEEEEE!
I SWEAR I'LL TAKE A BAT TO THAT PUNK.
GET OUT
AHH!

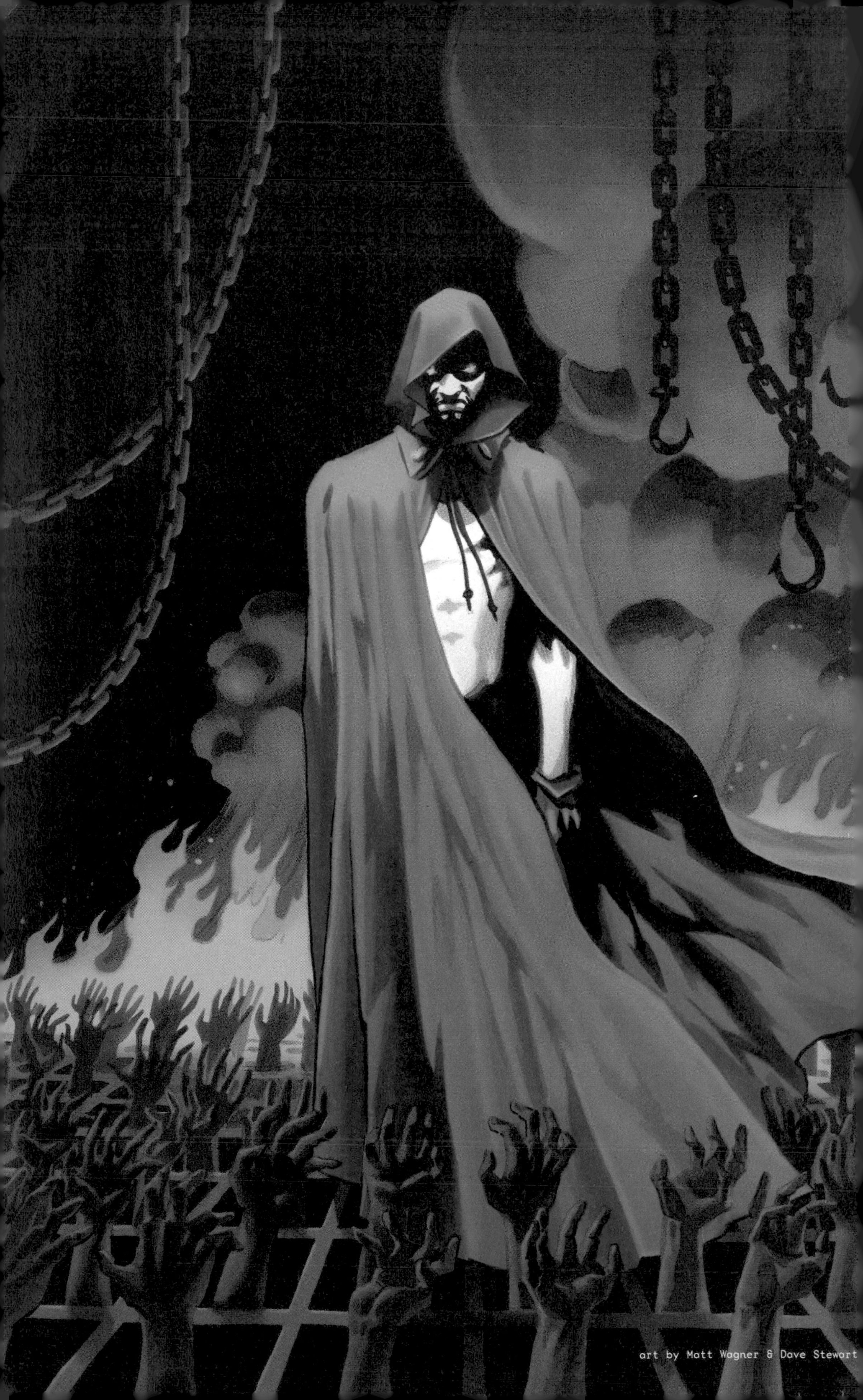

art by Matt Wagner & Dave Stewart

THIS IS *NOT* ALFONSO MUNOZ. IT'S HIS *YOUNGER* BROTHER *DAMIAN*.

IT WAS DAMIAN'S IDEA TO *CUT UP* HER AND HER TIGHT PANTS INTO *SMALL PIECES* AND FLUSH THEM DOWN THE TOILET.

ALFONSO HAS ALREADY MET *HIS* FATE.

WHEN ALFONSO WAS *THREE*, HIS OLDER COUSIN MADE HIM WATCH *JAWS* ON THE TELEVISION.

HE REFUSED TO TAKE A *BATH* FOR ALMOST A YEAR AND SOMETIMES HE *STILL* HAS *NIGHTMARES*.

OF COURSE, HE'S *NEVER* BEEN NEAR AN *OCEAN*.

IN HIS FINAL MOMENTS, THE *OCEAN* CAME TO HIM.

ALFONSO--!

GLUG

SSSHHHH

SLAM!

POLICE LINE DO NOT CROSS

GOLDSTEIN!

A **DRUG DEALER** AND A WOULD-BE **PSYCHOPATH** ARE GONE FROM THIS EARTH.

FINISHED WITH HIS UNIQUE BRAND OF **VENGEANCE**, THE SPECTRE GOES BACK FROM WHEREVER IT IS HE CAME.

LEAVING **CRISPUS ALLEN** TO ROOT ABOUT IN THE MESS.

DETECTIVE MARCUS DRIVER ARRIVES ON THE SCENE.

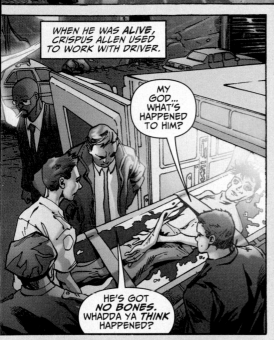

WHEN HE WAS **ALIVE**, CRISPUS ALLEN USED TO WORK WITH DRIVER.

MY GOD... WHAT'S HAPPENED TO HIM?

HE'S GOT **NO BONES**. WHADDA YA **THINK** HAPPENED?

HE KNOWS ALL OF DRIVER'S INSTINCTS ARE GOING OFF LIKE **ALARM BELLS**.

THIS IS THE **SIXTH** WHACKO CASE THIS **WEEK**. ONE MORE AND I'M **RETIRING**.

HE **KNOWS** THAT FEELING.

OF NEEDING TO FIND THAT **MISSING PIECE** THAT SETS EVERYTHING **RIGHT**.

NOW, ON THE **OTHER SIDE**, CRISPUS KNOWS **NONE** OF IT MATTERS.

THE ANSWERS DON'T CHANGE **ANYTHING**.

EVERY NIGHT HE GOES OUT AND FOLLOWS ANOTHER **DRUG DEALER**. ANOTHER **KILLER**.

EVERY NIGHT ANOTHER PIECE OF **HUMAN GARBAGE** IS REMOVED.

AND EVERY NIGHT, THERE'S **ANOTHER ONE** TO TAKE HIS PLACE.

AND EVERY DAY HE RETURNS HERE.

THE GRANVILLE TOWER APARTMENTS.

A MURDER WAS COMMITTED HERE, AND UNTIL HE UNCOVERS TH WHOLE TRUTH, HE'S DOOMED TO WANDER THESE HALLS.

HE FEELS AN OVERWHELMIN SENSE OF HA FOR THEM.

HE KNOWS HE SHOULDN'T.

BUT THESE PEOPLE HAVE NO DREAMS. NO HOPES.

THEY'VE BEEN THIS WAY LONG BEFORE THEIR SLUMLORD WAS STABBED TO DEATH IN THIS VERY HALLWAY.

IT'S CONSTANT. NEVER ENDING.

NOTHING BUT HATE.

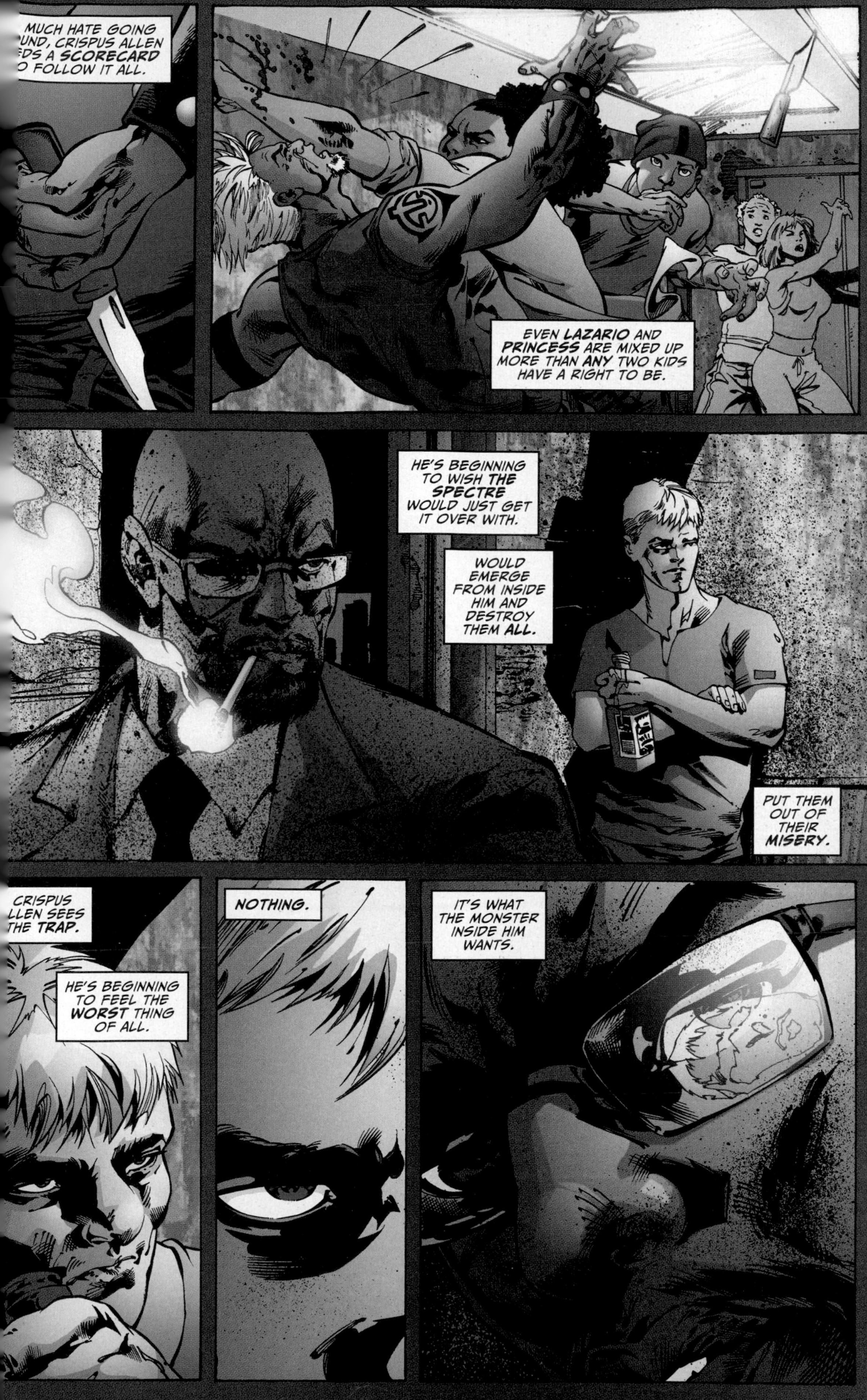
MUCH HATE GOING
UND, CRISPUS ALLEN
EDS A SCORECARD
O FOLLOW IT ALL.
EVEN LAZARIO AND PRINCESS ARE MIXED UP MORE THAN ANY TWO KIDS HAVE A RIGHT TO BE.
HE'S BEGINNING TO WISH THE SPECTRE WOULD JUST GET IT OVER WITH.
WOULD EMERGE FROM INSIDE HIM AND DESTROY THEM ALL.
PUT THEM OUT OF THEIR MISERY.
CRISPUS
LLEN SEES
THE TRAP.
HE'S BEGINNING TO FEEL THE WORST THING OF ALL.
NOTHING.
IT'S WHAT THE MONSTER INSIDE HIM WANTS.

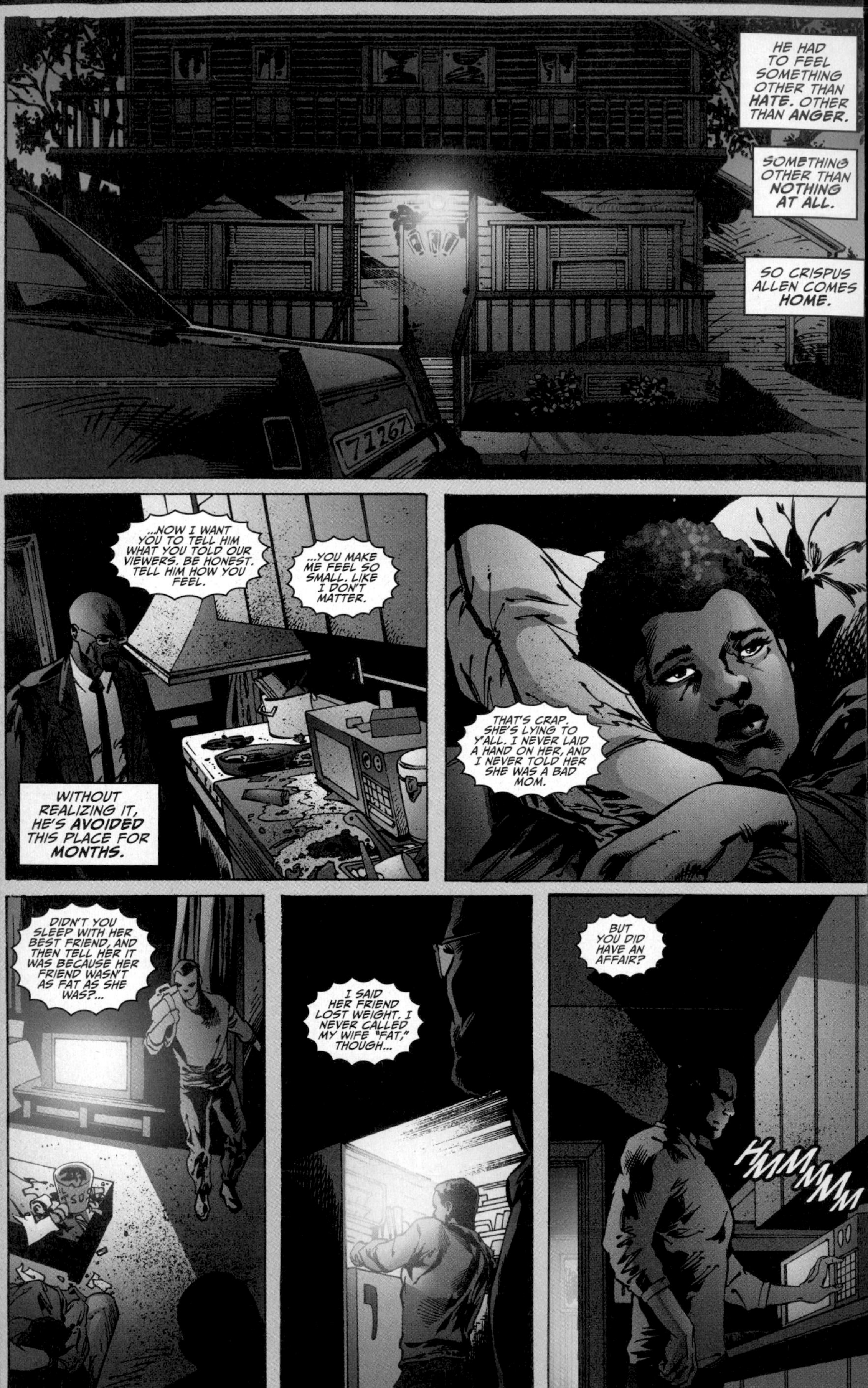
HE HAD TO FEEL SOMETHING OTHER THAN HATE. OTHER THAN ANGER.
SOMETHING OTHER THAN NOTHING AT ALL.
SO CRISPUS ALLEN COMES HOME.
...NOW I WANT YOU TO TELL HIM WHAT YOU TOLD OUR VIEWERS. BE HONEST. TELL HIM HOW YOU FEEL.
...YOU MAKE ME FEEL SO SMALL. LIKE I DON'T MATTER.
WITHOUT REALIZING IT, HE'S AVOIDED THIS PLACE FOR MONTHS.
THAT'S CRAP. SHE'S LYING TO Y'ALL. I NEVER LAID A HAND ON HER, AND I NEVER TOLD HER SHE WAS A BAD MOM.
DIDN'T YOU SLEEP WITH HER BEST FRIEND, AND THEN TELL HER IT WAS BECAUSE HER FRIEND WASN'T AS FAT AS SHE WAS?...
I SAID HER FRIEND LOST WEIGHT. I NEVER CALLED MY WIFE "FAT," THOUGH...
BUT YOU DID HAVE AN AFFAIR?
HMMMMMM

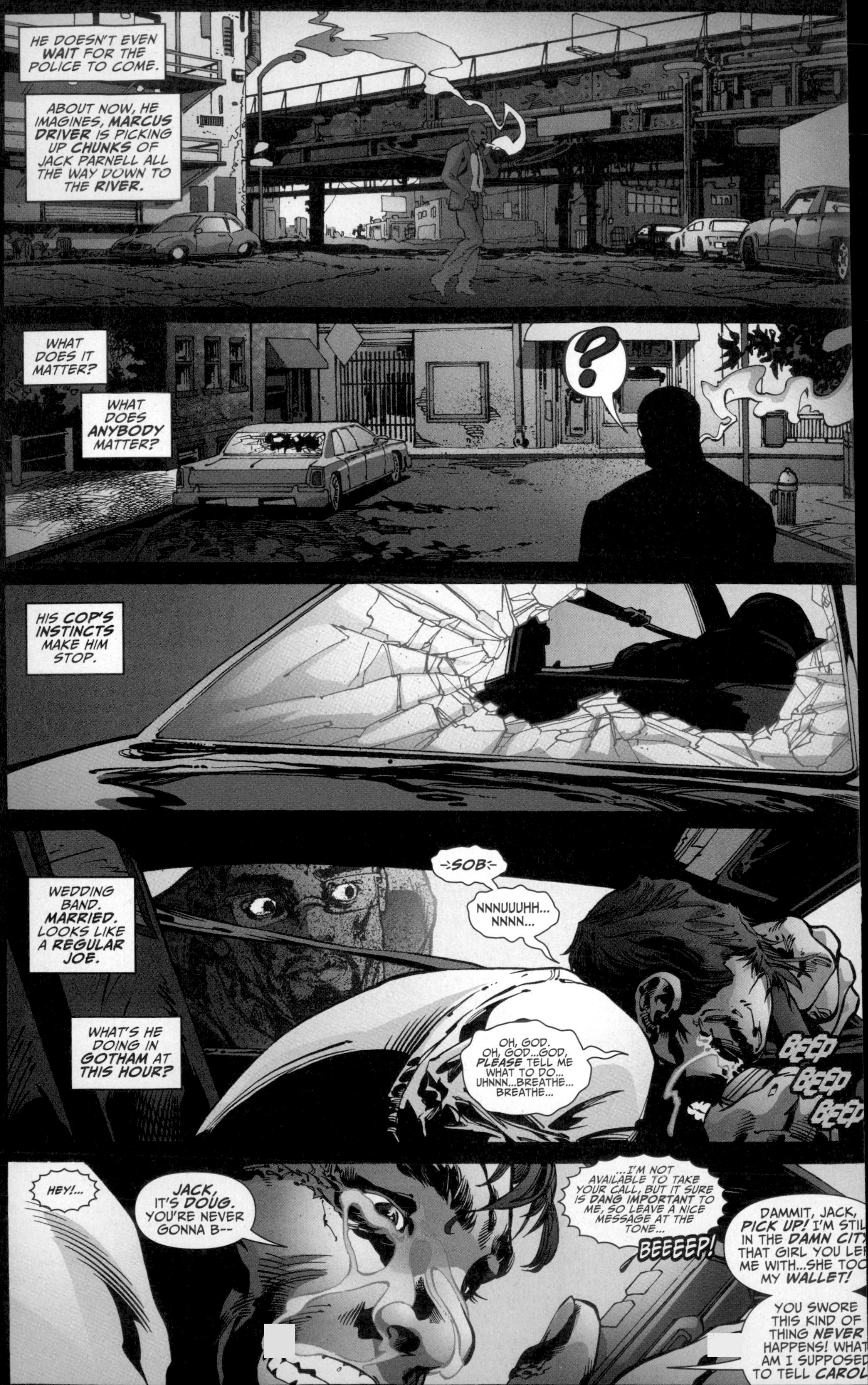

HE DOESN'T EVEN WAIT FOR THE POLICE TO COME.
ABOUT NOW, HE IMAGINES, MARCUS DRIVER IS PICKING UP CHUNKS OF JACK PARNELL ALL THE WAY DOWN TO THE RIVER.
WHAT DOES IT MATTER?
WHAT DOES ANYBODY MATTER?
?
HIS COP'S INSTINCTS MAKE HIM STOP.
WEDDING BAND. MARRIED. LOOKS LIKE A REGULAR JOE.
-SOB-
NNNUUUHH... NNNN...
WHAT'S HE DOING IN GOTHAM AT THIS HOUR?
OH, GOD. OH, GOD...GOD, PLEASE TELL ME WHAT TO DO... UHNNN...BREATHE... BREATHE...
BEEP
BEEP
BEEP
HEY!...
JACK, IT'S DOUG. YOU'RE NEVER GONNA B--
...I'M NOT AVAILABLE TO TAKE YOUR CALL, BUT IT SURE IS DANG IMPORTANT TO ME, SO LEAVE A NICE MESSAGE AT THE TONE...
BEEEEP!
DAMMIT, JACK, PICK UP! I'M STIL IN THE DAMN CITY THAT GIRL YOU LEF ME WITH...SHE TOO MY WALLET!
YOU SWORE THIS KIND OF THING NEVER HAPPENS! WHAT AM I SUPPOSED TO TELL CAROL

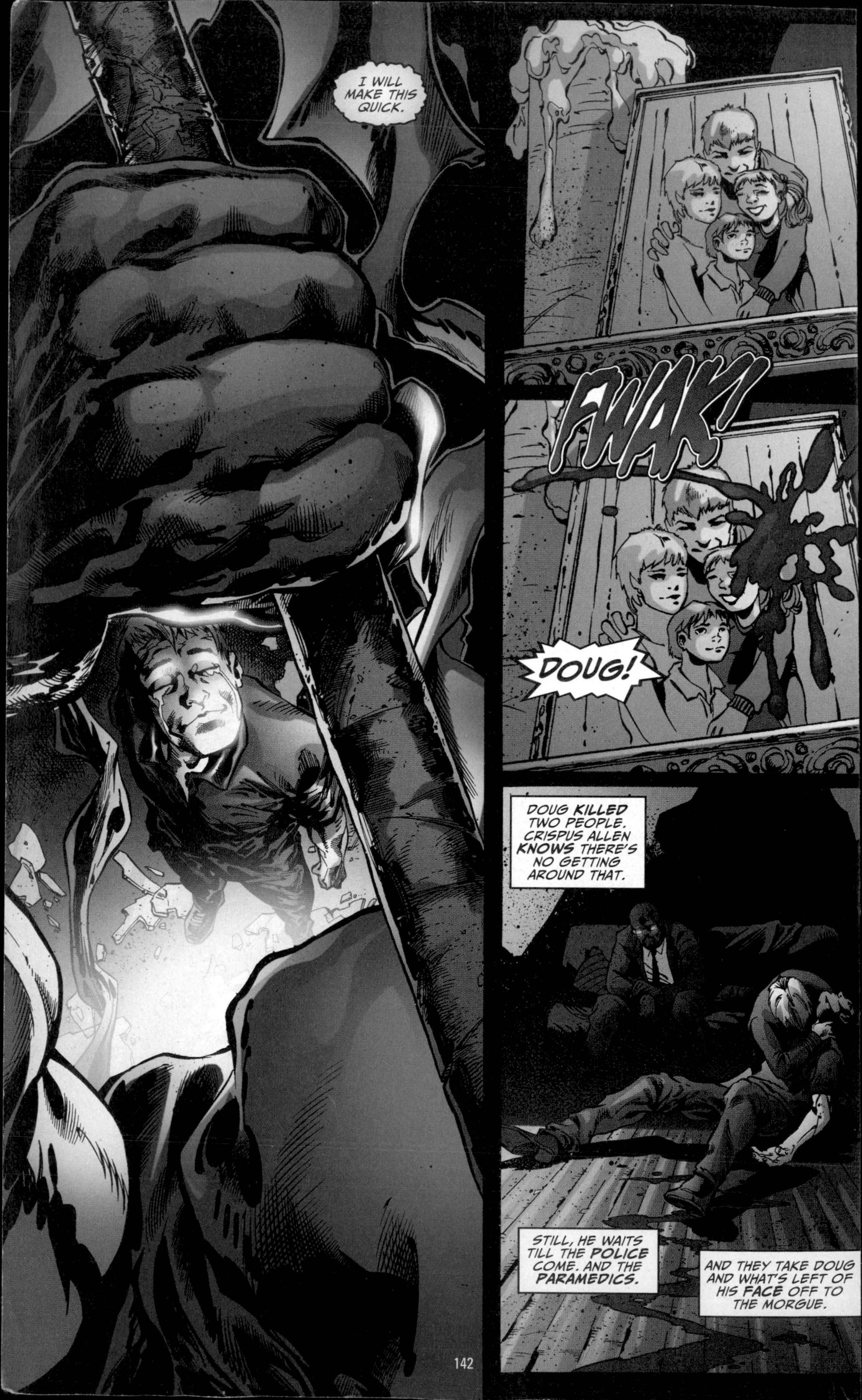
I WILL MAKE THIS QUICK.
FWAK!
DOUG!
DOUG KILLED TWO PEOPLE. CRISPUS ALLEN KNOWS THERE'S NO GETTING AROUND THAT.
STILL, HE WAITS TILL THE POLICE COME. AND THE PARAMEDICS.
AND THEY TAKE DOUG AND WHAT'S LEFT OF HIS FACE OFF TO THE MORGUE.

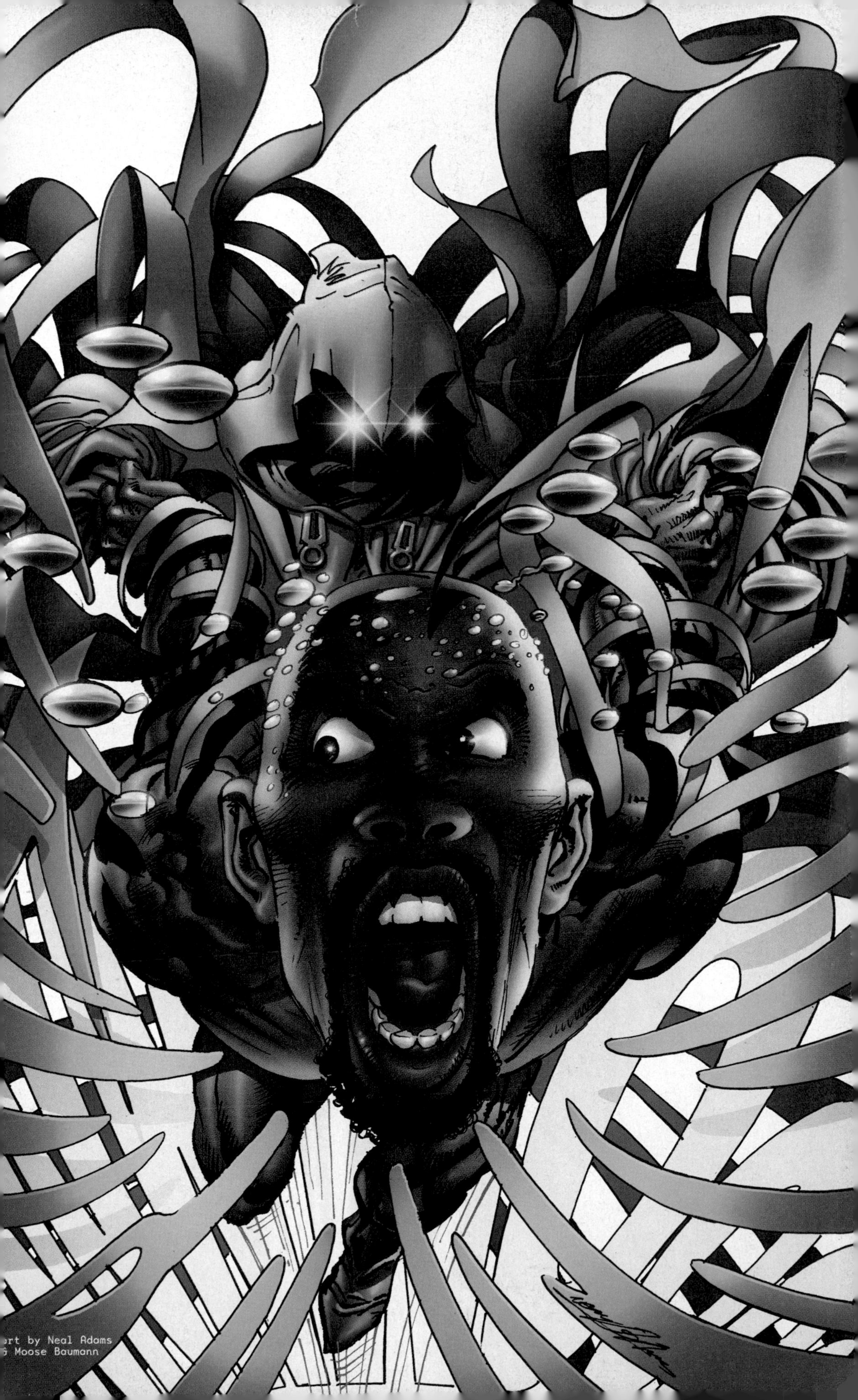

rt by Neal Adams
& Moose Baumann

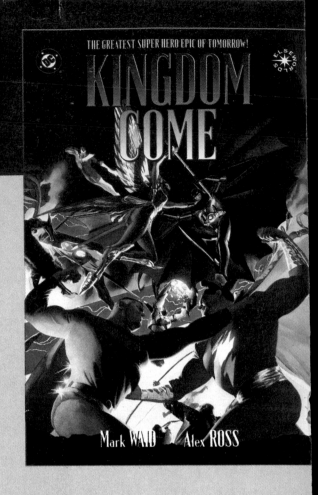
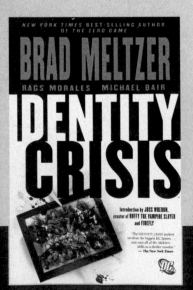